THE
ANGER TRAP

BOOKS BY ELIZABETH WEISS

Recovering From the Heart Attack Experience
From Female Depression to Contented Womanhood
Female Fatigue
The Female Breast
Protein Planner (with R. Wolfson)
Cookmates
Cholesterol Counter
Gourmet's Low Cholesterol Cookbook (with R. Wolfson)

THE
ANGER TRAP
Intimate Insights on Women's Anger

by

ELIZABETH WEISS

Philosophical Library
New York

All interviews in this book represent the real thoughts of real people. Due to their personal nature, the names and identities of those interviewed have been changed.

Library of Congress Cataloging in Publication Data

Weiss, Elizabeth S.
   The anger trap.

   1. Anger.   2. Women—Psychology.   I. Title.
BF575.A5W44   1984   152.4   84-1771
ISBN 0-8022-2452-0

Published 1984 by Philosophical Library, Inc.
200 West 57 Street, New York, N.Y. 10019.
Copyright 1984 by Elizabeth Weiss.
All rights reserved.
Manufactured in the United States of America.

To Stan, Gregory and Mark
Who teach me daily about anger...
and love

CONTENTS

Acknowledgments

Anger is an intimate feeling. For two years, I have interviewed scores of women. They have been married, single, divorced and widowed. Most had children, several were childless. They were from very different social, economic and religious backgrounds but they shared one crucial trait. They were all honest. They have exposed their real thoughts and feelings to me and for this I am exceedingly grateful to:

Selma Affatey, Susan Bemish, Roberta Burkan, Barbara Cohen, Kathleen Downing, Rochelle Edelson, Rena Grossman, Linda Jacoby, Helen Kellert, Carolyn Krinsley, Fran Lande, Phyllis Makofsky, Elise Meyer, Gracia Milittauer, Thea Millstein, Joan Nevins, Nancy Pasternack, Rosalie Popper, Jane Rosenbloom, Joan Rosner, Joanne Rosoff, Alison Vincent, Rona Woldenberg and the women of the Manhattan Plaza Mothering Center.

ix

The life experiences and feelings of others can comfort us. They can only enlighten us in combination with psychological knowledge. For their professional insights and psychiatric explanations, I am deeply indebted to:

Madelaine Amiel, M.D., Iris Ascher, M.D., Harriet Berchenko, Anna Burton, M.D., Patricia Schreiner-Engle, Ph.D., Sheila Jackman, M.D., Ned Marcus, M.D., David Novick, M.D., Andrew Looker, M.D., Mary Sams, Ph.D., Raymond Simon, M.D. and Irma Zelig, M.D.

Writing a book is a challenging but immensely difficult task. Without the help of two friends, it would not have been nearly as enjoyable nor fulfilling. For their willing assistance, I would like to thank David Mills, who gave me a wonderful place in which to work, and Georgina Searle, whose willingness to type and retype helped me clarify my presentation.

Lastly, but in my thoughts primarily, I would also like to thank my husband, Stan, and my sons, Mark and Gregory. Their emotional support and constant encouragement have enabled me to try to combine family responsibilities and a career. It is, I know well, impossible to do everything. For putting up with my impatience, excusing my inattention to housekeeping chores and most of all, for allowing me to be angry when I felt like it, I am deeply grateful to them.

Introduction

"A New York University professor's wife methodically murdered her two young children in their posh East Side apartment today, then killed herself with a shotgun she bought earlier for $89.

"A maid found the pajama-clad body of Mrs. Irene Schwartz, 36.

"Her children, Joshua, 7, and Judy, 5, were sprawled across their mother's blood-soaked bed.... Each child lay on either side of the mother's body...."

In startled horror I read this in the *New York Post* on September 10, 1980. I knew Irene Schwartz. Her daughter Judy was in my son Mark's class. They went to camp together. Judy had played at our house many times. I saw Irene each morning when I took Mark to school. I had coffee at her house. And many times, we had talked.

Irene seemed just like me; just like so many other young New York City mothers. We were all fixing up our apartments, wondering about our careers and taking care of our children. If there was any noticeable difference between Irene and the rest of the "Blue Room" mothers, perhaps it was only that Irene was serene. She seemed at peace. She was never impatient with her children. She never yelled at them. In a word, she never showed anger.

Like most of her friends, I found the tragedy of Irene Schwartz haunting. If Irene could do such a violent thing, why not me? Why not any of us?

An intimate insight into women's anger seemed badly needed.

In my own life, I knew anger was too frequently felt but infrequently expressed. Did other women—like my friend Judy—also feel rage they feared to express? How could I better manage my own hidden-from-the-world angers? This book contains the answers I found.

It is not meant as a textbook of psychiatry nor a book to use until the psychiatrist comes. It is neither a recommendation nor a condemnation of professional help. It is not a defense of anger in the women's movement. But it is, I hope, a book which reflects how women today really feel—what really happens inside their homes and, even more intimately, inside their hearts.

We are not always able to see ourselves clearly; the feelings and experience of others helps gives us insight. By understanding the sources of our anger and the ways we, without even realizing it, manage our anger, we will be better able to use this emotion to enhance, rather than destroy, ourselves and those we love.

1

Are You Angry?

"Just ask me, I'm an expert in the topic."
"You've sure asked the right person."
"So many things make me angry, I don't know where to begin."

That's the way most women responded when I said I was writing on women and anger. All women—even beautiful women, successful women, patient women and take-charge types—have anger. So this book is about all of us. It is about the things that make us angry and how we can focus this feeling for the benefit, rather than destruction, of ourselves and those most important to us.

"At the age of thirty-nine, I am still learning the benefits of getting angry spontaneously," an airline personnel assistant explained. "In an effort to keep a man around, I never wanted to make waves. A lot of my anger went unexpressed or I really toned it down. I was so afraid that my partner wouldn't like me

1

anymore. He might go away and leave me."

A thirty-eight-year-old mother of three explained, "My husband, David, has a volatile temper. I'm afraid to tell him my honest feelings because I'm scared he'll just explode and walk out. So I keep quiet but I feel furious inside. I think a lot of anger has to do with being afraid and feeling insecure."

Most women hide their anger for one overwhelming reason: fear of the loss of love. They are afraid their anger will make them unloveable. So they gulp it back down and keep it with the one person they know will stick around: themselves.

Even in an intimate relationship, many women are never really themselves, never completely relaxed. They never totally let down their hair. Fearing the consequences of their anger, they tell themselves:

"If I start something, things might get out of my control."
"If I act sweet and nice, he'll never know I'm angry."
"I don't want to make a mountain out of a molehill."
"I'll wait until a better time to 'say something.' "
"I just want to keep everyone happy."

They try to hide their anger, saying instead, "I'm so annoyed," "I'm tense," or "I'm under a lot of stress." "I feel so upset" is perhaps the commonest subterfuge. The word "upset" is often used as a substitute for "angry." Whatever the excuse, however—even if the suppression is completely unconscious—anger accumulates. Insidiously, it affects our relationships even if we don't want it to.

Sometimes women do not even realize they are angry. A vague, diffuse dissatisfaction is often the feeling when we are chronically angry but don't know it. To see if you are angry—too angry for good emotional health—take this simple test:

1. Do you feel angry most of the time?

2. Are you afraid to express your true feelings because it might destroy a crucial relationship?
3. Do you find you talk about trivial things because when you try to say something important, you always feel rejected or put down?
4. Do you find yourself consciously hiding anger, keeping angry secrets?
5. When faced with another person's anger, do you try to quickly drop the issue rather than face the conflict head-on?
6. Do you avoid little blow-ups to "keep the peace"?
7. Do you express your anger only when it is safe, for example with people unable to express it back?
8. Do you use the "silent treatment" when you are really angry?
9. Do you find you are ready to do battle at the drop of a hat, not to mention a word or inconvenience?
10. Do you often feel depressed, pervasively unhappy, trapped?
11. Are you hesitant to express yourself because you are always being labeled a "nag," "troublemaker," or "bitch?"
12. Do you wish you could be more open with your feelings?

If you answered "yes" to eight or more, you probably have too much hidden anger.

A good test of whether you've been successful in expressing your anger is to note whether your angry feelings dissipate. After you express your anger, you should feel better, more satisfied and no longer angry. But if you are angry and also confused and in a lot of conflict, or when you try to unload everything that's bothering you onto one person, it probably won't work. Scapegoating and aggressively thrashing around in a misdirected fashion just makes you angrier.

Another self-analysis: If the amount of feeling coming out of you seems proportionate to the issue at hand, you are probably handling your anger in a healthy way. When your feelings are excessive, however, you are probably tapping a reservoir of repressed old angers and resentments.

Most often, women keep their anger to themselves because they are afraid of losing a much-needed relationship. In a word, they feel desperate.

Janice Jones was typical of many, many women. For her, Tom was not just a need, he was her entire life. Absolutely everything rode on their relationship. When Tom left, it seemed Janice's will to live left with him. As she explained: "I was madly in love with Tom. He was everything I ever wanted. When I was with him, I felt great. My life had meaning. But when he walked out, I ached all over. Nothing made me happy. My sorrow and hurt were indescribable. It has been three years and I still feel totally empty inside. I'm a walking shell."

We are all dependent on others. Love relationships entail dependency. But the degree varies. The excessively dependent woman feels totally helpless, unable to live without a sustaining husband or lover, unable to build any life on her own. Such women are afraid that expressing anger will drive away this desperately needed partner.

Many dependent women have deep-seated feelings of inferiority from childhood. Due to this insecurity, the dependent woman usually swallows her anger. Even when she expresses anger, her choice of target is often inappropriate. And her anger may become totally out of control. She may feel someone is holding her back in some way. "Look what you are making me do," is the feeling. It is much like a child who feels mistreated and wants revenge. Unfortunately, these methods only succeed in pushing people further away.

The more deeply dependent a woman is, the more repressed her anger is likely to be. Not only is her security at stake, her whole sense of self can be wiped away. Silence is safe. If she begins to speak, she fears an angry and turbulent truth might inadvertently emerge which could greatly harm her. It could loosen her from her life raft.

"Most of the good and positive things this kind of individual has in her life," explained Dr. Malcolm Bowers, Chief of Psychiatry at Yale-New Haven Hospital, "come from other people—and most frequently from the affection and approval of some crucial other person. If this relationship is threatened, the emotionally dependent individual may feel her very being to be in jeopardy."

The dependent person is so fearful, she exchanges power and responsibility for "someone to lean on." But trade-offs might not be what we expect. As one twenty-eight-year-old black woman explained, "When I first got married, I didn't work. Every penny I had came from my husband. I always had to ask him and he wasn't always willing to give. On the other hand, it was his money and he could do whatever he felt like with it.

"The blow came when I wanted to go to a party. I wanted to buy a new dress and I asked him for money. His answer was 'no.' It wasn't a lot of money—maybe fifty dollars. He had it but he just wouldn't give it to me. Never, never again would I put myself in the situation where I had to beg. I was furious. Over and over, in my marriage I learned—when you are totally dependent on someone, they always let you down...always."

Excessive dependency eventually makes the receiver resentful and angry. Another person has too much control. The giver also becomes resentful, constantly burdened with someone else's weight. And dependency usually brings disappointment. As Diane Von Furstenberg, the dress designer and author, advised: "The more you are in control of your life, the better. All your days, until you die, you have only one constant companion—yourself. Depend only on yourself and you won't be disappointed."

When dependency makes it too threatening for a woman to

express her anger directly, she may transfer the anger onto a safer object. Psychiatrists call this *displacement*. Victims of a lifelong rage at their mothers may transfer this feeling to a husband. While some people may be aware of displacing their anger, many times it is completely subconscious. Such anger, once expressed, becomes exaggerated. This is because it is an accumulation of old angers. Also there is resentment, often subconscious, that the anger had to be hidden originally.

Exaggerations and accumulations can sometimes be quite violent. The anger often becomes chronic. Nothing is more destructive of human relationships. These people are inappropriately angry most of the time because their anger is never resolved.

"I'm so frustrated, I could cry," women often say. Tears may be a subconscious attempt to avoid anger. What we are really feeling is, "I'm furious but I'm totally impotent to do anything about it." Interestingly, tears are less likely to appear when anger can be expressed openly.

"We should vent our feelings," we are told. Unfortunately, this can sometimes produce more agony than relief.

At one time or another, everyone has "roared like a maniac," discharging anger in an impulsive, intense outburst. Others may have labeled it "infantile" or called us "a real bitch." Most likely, the result was only rejection and more powerlessness. To have anger work *for*, rather than against us, we must understand certain facts about anger.

1. ANGER DOES NOT KILL A RELATIONSHIP.

As one woman confessed to us, "I'm afraid to tell my husband how I really feel because I think the honesty would shine too bright a light on the whole relationship. When things are spelled out too clearly, there is no 'unsaying' things. I don't think the relationship could take it."

Many women have this "don't make waves" attitude. Their entire personalities are based on being "nice." They fear anger will kill love and most of us cannot live without love.

Anger will kill the kind of neurotic love that cannot take the least strain. But this is not love at all; it is neurotic dependency. This type of relationship will probably be destroyed, despite all of our attempts, because strain is inevitable. Meaningful love—love which lasts—is actually strengthened by anger. It reunites a couple. Indeed, a certain amount of anger is necessary for intimacy.

2. ANGER ENABLES US TO "FORGIVE AND FORGET." ✓

Anger must be experienced for forgiving and forgetting to take place. Forgiving and forgetting are extremely important for healthy relationships. Without them, personal hurt and anger go on and on destroying all possibility for closeness. Unexpressed anger creates emotional distance.

3. GETTING ANGRY IS NEITHER RIGHT NOR WRONG.

Again and again, women will ask, "I was right to get angry, wasn't I?" Justice has no bearing on anger. It doesn't have to be logical. People who seek justifications are attempting to excuse something they feel is basically wrong. Anger is neither right nor wrong. It is a feeling we have and therefore we have the right to express it. It is much like feeling hungry. If someone has just eaten and still feels hungry, she has a feeling of hunger, no matter what we say. Anger is the same. Once anger is felt—regardless of whether it is justified or not—we should be able to talk about it.

4. ANGER HAPPENS TO BOTH YOUNG AND OLD.

Anger is a common feeling in adults and children alike. Some parents equate "goodness in children" with a lack of anger. "I remember getting very angry at my mother when I was about eight," one woman recalled. "I got up all my courage and tried to hit her. My mother blanched and said you must never, never do that again. She made me feel like I was the worst girl that ever lived, the only little girl evil enough to try to hit her own mother."

Some people feel adults should "control their anger." They believe it shows immaturity to "fly off the handle." The way anger is expressed may, indeed, be immature. It may be inappropriate (more constructive approaches will be given later). However, the recognition and expression of this feeling is a sign of maturity, not immaturity.

5. IF YOU DEADEN ANGER, YOU KILL LOVE.

Many women, raised to be "good little girls," try to feel only "good" feelings. Of course, this attempted selection is never really possible. You may think it works but the anger eventually poisons, despite our best efforts. As Dr. Theodore Isaac Rubin, past president of the American Institute of Psychoanalysis, explains, "Sitting on a feeling effects a freeze up, which gradually encroaches on all feelings, and even obliteration.... Anger and love do not operate in separate compartments. We cannot reject one and hope to experience the other. An insult to one will invariably produce repercussions in the other."

Fascinating scientific experiments show the importance of anger in relationships. In a famous series, Dr. Harry Harlow of the University of Wisconsin reared monkeys. Harlow's calm, mechanical, totally accepting and non-fighting monkey mothers raised offspring who grew up "normal except that they couldn't and wouldn't make love."

Another distinguished researcher, Konrad Lorenz, made similar observations from bird experiments. He stated, "Among birds, the most aggressive representatives of any group are also the staunchest friends, and the same applies to mammals. To the best of our knowledge, bond behavior does not exist except in aggressive organisms." Sociologist Dr. Erik Erikson of Harvard University blames the failure to achieve human intimacy on "the inability to engage in controversy and useful combat."

Are you angry? we asked at the outset of this chapter. It seems like an easy "yes" or "no." Certainly, we should know how we ourselves feel. Yet many people who are angry will have no genuine awareness of their anger or will completely misinterpret anger for another emotion. Psychiatrists say it is not uncommon to hear a clearly angry person talk about feeling "anxious."

People are confused about what to do with anger, even when it is recognized. The problem is that expressing anger can turn others off. It can bring rejection.

How can you handle this double bind? In the late 1970's, the "emotion as pus" or "let it all hang out" theories abounded. The idea was to bring anger to a head and then discharge it through any means—cathartic howling or even screaming. Simply discharging anger, however, does not alleviate it.

Unfortunately, there are no easy answers or convenient formulas. But dealing with anger wisely is essential. This is, in fact, so true that many psychiatrists believe how a person handles anger indicates their entire mental health. Through anger insight, we can improve our relationships and, most importantly, enhance our own self-esteem.

2

Why Women?

Over and over professionals reported they were seeing a tremendous amount of anger in women. They found:

Women were angrier and more bitter than men.
Women were angrier at men than men were at women.
Women were more discontented with their world than men were with theirs.
Women, more than men, wanted revenge.

Why? Myths are part of the answer. Dr. Leah Schaefer, a psychotherapist and author of *Women and Sex*, has stated:

"A woman's life is filled with fantasies. You have the fantasy of the kind of man you think your father is and the fantasy of what your mother says he is. You have the fantasy of the kind of man you think you should marry and the fantasy of the kind of man you actually do marry. You have a fantasy of what life is going to be like. A lot of us end up not being able to cope with the reality of our lives because we always have that fantasy in our mind of what it should have been."

Many women not only want a certain type of marriage and family, they expect it. When they face a very different reality, they feel cheated, frustrated and very angry. For solutions, they usually look to externals, feeling, "If only I had a child...," or "If only my husband had a better job...," or "If only my child was smart...," or "If only we lived in a nice house." The problem is, even when these wishes are fulfilled, others always come to take their place. This is because our real discontent and anger may be in and at ourselves.

Unsatisfying relationships can also make a woman feel unloved and unnurtured, raw and alone. Lashing out angrily is often a response to hurt.

One forty-five-year-old mother of three explained, "I've noticed men and women get angry differently. For example, my husband really blows. Two minutes later, it's like nothing ever happened. When I get angry, I broil inside. Five days later, something trivial will make me explode."

Many women fear getting angry because they are afraid of being abandoned. When a person is angry, they experience a sense of separateness from the person they are confronting. For many women, this precipitates a "separation anxiety." Although we may not consciously be aware of it, we may feel a need to quickly "get back" the person we are angry with. This leads women to cry, apologize or prematurely "make peace." In this way, we assure an important "other" will not abandon us and leave us all alone. The trouble with this conciliatory stance is there are psychological costs. Our anger, not properly resolved, may grow.

A forty-year-old law student we interviewed, in explaining her own divorce, reiterated the destructiveness of "making peace" without real resolution.

"I got really angry and very unhappy that first year in law school and began thinking about things I'd resented for a long time that I'd never expressed. Well, I think it's the double whammy, this thing of not letting yourself get angry. I think that we often don't let ourselves realize that we're angry and resentful, and I found that as I spoke about my present anger, past resentments would come out as well; things that I had not even spent that much time thinking about consciously.

"I got to the point of feeling such seething that I knew I just had to get out of there—or go crazy. The anger took me over physically. At the time, it got so bad, it was a very physical feeling that I had to go. There were an awful lot of pressures that were just too much to deal with. We'd had a history of moving a lot. It was something I really didn't want to do. It was very stressful and difficult. I really think a lot of my problems could have been eliminated if I'd acknowledged feelings to myself and then expressed them, instead of strangling on them and having them suddenly erupt."

Security is a subtle thing. It is a feeling of acceptance for our whole selves, with all our good parts and bad. Acceptance is conveyed in the way we treat each other, which, almost unconsciously, reveals our true feelings. If we do not feel complete approval, we will not express our real feelings honestly and openly. We will hold back to protect ourselves.

One mother of three explained: "When I talk to my husband, he never seems 'there.' I always get the feeling he wants me to hurry up and finish. He seems to judge me negatively as I speak. It makes me not want to tell him things."

Nearly all of us have a special set of senses that measure the way people listen to us when we talk. They work like this: As we speak, words go out and simultaneously the speaker receives a reaction. Sometimes these reactions are "I see," "Yes," or simply "Hmm." Or they may be negative reactions, "Oh no," "Why's that?" But these are only the spoken reactions.

The more important reactions are fleeting visual clues. A man's face may brighten up just slightly to show he approves. He may smile, nod, or move slightly forward. All of these things show that our words are being well received.

However, when a man looks away from his mate, he gives the signal something is wrong. He may screw up his face, or scowl, even without realizing it. He may shake his head. There are hundreds of visual clues—some almost invisible—that convey meaning from listener to talker. If the reactions are good, they have the effect of loosening her up, of allowing her to talk freely. If the reactions are negative, the road is rough for the person talking. Almost automatically, she struggles to overcome the bad reactions. These reactions cause a person to stop talking.

The importance of a return reaction when we speak is more important to our talking effectively than most of us realize. By the way people respond, they actually control to a large degree the communication that will occur. If the attention of the listener wanders, something inside the talker dies. There is a tremendous desire to cut things short and withdraw.

Unfortunately, many of the reactions that a talker observes in a listener cannot be produced artificially. They are not mannerisms that can be practiced. All the reactions—good or bad—are symptoms of the human attitude behind them. If we have positive attitudes towards the person talking, the visible reactions will take care of themselves. On the other hand, if the listener has a critical view, this will be transmitted.

For most women, their husband is their only continuous listener. If he is not a sympathetic and supportive listener, the woman is left alone with thoughts that can boil up inside until there is immense anger. With a good listener, troublesome thoughts can often be talked into nothingness.

If supportive listening is not offered by a spouse, a woman will seek it from someone. She may phone one friend after another; or she may turn to another man—one who listens.

Perhaps the first and foremost lesson in becoming a good listener is to take the time to listen. When you sense that someone wants to talk, don't put it off. Don't wait for a more convenient time. Take the time, then and there, if at all possible.

It is also very important not to assume you know what another person is thinking. Correcting a person's statement of his or her own feelings is infuriating and will just intensify the anger.

A woman does not hide her anger because of an unsupportive partner alone. Society pressures women to be silent. While men and women are equally capable of expressing their anger, for centuries there has been a taboo about women expressing anger. Lest anyone think this is something new, it is fascinating to note that the first written laws, dating to approximately 2500 B.C., decreed that a woman who was verbally abusive to her husband was to have her name engraved on a brick, which would then be used to knock out her teeth!

We cannot completely blame men for women's reticence. Women themselves have contributed to the myth. Biologically, women are not subservient to men. They have fifty percent less muscle mass but a longer life expectancy (at age eighty-five, women outnumber men two to one). Emotionally, women are not weaker—in the first six months after a spouse's death more widowers than widows die. Yet many mothers have raised their daughters to feel weak.

A twenty-four-year-old costume designer recalls, "I was raised to believe I couldn't do 'it'...whatever 'it' was. It makes me unable to make decisions today. I always think, 'I can't really do that.' My husband never asks himself, 'Can I do that?' But I pose the question to myself constantly."

While women have always been allowed to express anger in defense of others—the young, weak or old—their own anger has been treated as unladylike, even illegitimate. More than anything, this is probably due to fear. To appreciate the intensity of this fear, we must remember that all of us spent our critical years in the arms of a woman. Each of us was completely dependent on a mother not only for nurturance and well-being but for our very life. Therefore, children have deep love for the mother but also deep anger at her power and control. Children's fairy tales reflect this: We see the omnipotent Fairy Godmother possessing inexhaustible powers of good and the frightening wicked stepmother able to destroy all in her path.

"So I'm angry, I'll admit it. What can I do about it?" A woman might ask. We all identify with the sources of anger. What is the solution? To have anger work *for*, rather than against us, it is helpful to keep in mind these basic dos and don'ts:

DO:

ACKNOWLEDGE THAT ANGER EXISTS. The more you are aware of the anger in you, the better chance you have of using it beneficially. No one lives anger-free. Acknowledge this feeling and try to express it forthrightly.

PINPOINT THE PROBLEM. Many women know that they are angry but they do not know the exact source of this feeling. Sources may be difficult to identify if the real instigator is someone who is powerful or could harm us. We may think we know the source but this is just the object we have displaced the anger upon. An important clue is more anger towards a situation than is realistically warranted. One should then suspect that the real anger is at something or someone else.

TRY TO EXPRESS ANGER DIRECTLY. If you get angry but hide it, the message will still get across. When there is a direct exchange, it can be openly discussed and resolved. Indirectly anger gives no possibility for resolution.

DON'T:

FOCUS ON FAIRNESS. "It's all so unfair," women cry. There are a lot of unfair things that happen to women (and men, too). Some are caused by circumstances; others by people. Particularly when relationships end, women often feel things have been unfair. We get angrier and angrier trying to make others see and really understand all the unfairness. Most of us know we cannot stop others from being "unfair" but we have trouble actually accepting that fact. This can produce so much anger, it can easily overwhelm us, sapping all our energy.

PURPOSELY RECALL HURTFUL EVENTS. Particularly when a person's feelings have been badly hurt, it is not unusual to think over and over about other hurtful past events. One hurt seems to remind us of other, older hurts. We begin to recall all the injustices of our entire life, from early childhood on. This causes more anger than is possible to resolve. One cannot forget but we can turn the page on past hurts and begin each day, as nature does, anew.

3

Childhood: Where It All Begins

We learn how to read. We are taught how to write. No one gives us lessons in expressing our anger. But we learn. We learn it very well. The lessons are with us for life.

All human beings are born with the ability to feel and express anger. The things that make us angry and the way we respond to our anger are not inborn. They are learned. As children we learn ways of expressing our emotions from those around us—our parents, our brothers and sisters. We respond to the feeling in our home. A healthy home is one where—first and foremost—all emotions, even anger, are given ample freedom. There is no holding back. All emotions are openly expressed and exchanged. "Bad" emotions are not excluded and only "good emotions" allowed. In such a home, it is easy to know what people feel. And it is easy to express your emotions because you know they will be accepted. Nothing needs to be stifled. You can be yourself without fear. You are safe.

Unfortunately, in some homes, parents feel one way but act another. The double message does the damage.

A thwarted child may shout at her mother, "I hate you." Angry, the mother may shout back, "Don't talk to me like that." If the mother, inevitably angry, turns to the child and in an unnaturally calm voice says, "I'm not angry at you; I just don't like how you behave," there is a double message. The child may think, "You seem angry; I can feel it," but the words she hears contradict this. Confused, the child is not sure how to reply or behave. An honest message calms and reassures us. But a double message blows up small incidents to giant proportions, causing conflict, anxiety and great stores of anger.

Such tiny dramas, when we were very young, live on in us. Years later, present incidents reverberate against these long ago experiences. As adults, we find ourselves wondering, "If I'm angry, will he still love me?" Feeling angry, we hear ourselves saying, "Everything is fine."

Diana, a thirty-nine-year-old history teacher, told how double messages during childhood affected her.

"We never yelled in our family because it's not a nice thing to do. People went off to weep alone in their rooms because you didn't want to upset anyone. There was a lot of second guessing. If I wanted to do something but my mother didn't approve she would say, 'If that's what will make you happy, dear.' Translated this, of course, meant she thought it was a terrible idea. There was a need to continually translate. If I said, 'Ah, you don't think I should,' she would counter with, 'Didn't I just say it was okay?' This type of exchange always left me confused and mistrustful—especially of the positive things. 'That's a good idea' could really mean, 'that's a terrible idea.' You were never sure."

Children naturally express their anger openly. They hit, bite, yell, spit and swear. And they cry. Anger is felt by all children. It is, in large measure, due to dependence.

Yet some parents equate "goodness in children" with a lack of anger. They tell their "good little girls" to always "be nice." This implies that a child should never get angry. Of course, the child still gets angry. But she hides it, as if it were dirty. She begins pretending. Her emotional freedom ends.

Jane Jacobs, a social worker, knows very well the danger of such nice-girl admonitions:

> "I've had a lot of trouble with anger as an adult because I was told as a very young child, you are not supposed to be angry. You are supposed to be nice. But I was immensely angry at my own mother. I wanted to kill her. I never wanted to make anyone angry with me because I was afraid they may have the same feelings I had. They might, in their heart, wish to kill me...."

One twenty-five-year-old typist explained her situation this way:

> "My parents were divorced when I was six months old. As a child, any time I would get angry, my mother would say, 'Just like your father!' Or she would say, 'What's *wrong* with you?' as if there was some odd abnormality that was causing this strange feeling. Of course, I got angry anyway but I could never show it. It would build up. Finally, I would fly off into a rage and have an uncontrollable tantrum."

(Psychiatrists say a child's temper tantrum is often an effort to upset the parents, thus an indirect satisfaction of their anger at the parents.)

In some homes, there is no real emotional interaction. What may look like strong emotional displays are actually superficial outbursts. These involve small issues, larger difficulties being silently but scrupulously avoided. Such sudden outbursts just give way to more inhibition. And so the pattern goes.

At times, anger can be due to a parent who was particularly cruel. Janice, whose parents divorced when she was twelve, has felt a deep abiding anger at her father.

"My father was in the service when I was born. He didn't see me until I was two years old. He left a childless bride and came back to a child who didn't know him. From that moment on, I resented him and he resented me. He was very mean and nasty. When he had a temper tantrum, he would throw lamps. He hit me with a fork at the dinner table. Once when I spilled peas on the table, he made me eat peas off the floor. If I sniffled at church, he would pinch me so hard I cried, but no one could see what he was doing.

"He was a very rigid person, a real churchgoer. Every Sunday, I was slow as a poke getting ready for church. It would make him furious and he would turn to real nastiness.

"Of course when we got to church or with his colleagues, he was totally different. He told me once I was dumb as a goose, then two minutes later when he saw his friends he said, 'Oh, my lovely daughter!'

"When I was little and he was big, he scared the cheese out of me. He did demeaning things, unfair things, cruel things. He'd tell me I was a worm, that I caused his arguing with my mother, that I caused all the fighting in the family. These are destructive things to do to a child. I have never forgiven him."

A lack of understanding from parents increases the anger children feel. This often reaches a crescendo during adolescence. Margeaux James, a twenty-year-old college junior and English major, vividly recalls her own adolescent confusions:

"When I was thirteen years old, I thought about suicide 'cause I didn't get along with my parents and the people at school. It was such a social scene.

"I was really shy. Now the whole thing makes me angry; but then, I felt like such an outsider. My parents didn't understand. I'd come home from school, take out all my problems on my parents, and they'd get mad at me.

"I'd storm from the dinner table, slam my door, throw pencils across my room, and then cry. In a way, I was afraid of it. You know, first base, second base, and all that crap. If you did it, everyone knew. There was no privacy.

"My friends alluded to sex and 'affairs' with guys, but they were really so upright. 'If she goes to bed with someone, she's a whore,' was what they really thought.

"Guys would even lie about how far they'd gone with a girl. Some guy came up to me and said, 'I heard you went to second with John.' I was so shy and turned beet red. It was probably anger, but I didn't know how to deal with it. I've always had a hard time getting angry, so I'd get embarrassed instead. I wish I could do it all over. I'd talk to my parents. Then, I felt totally out of control of the situation. It was a vicious circle. I hated myself."

What is the solution to all this long ago anger? The answer is not to call up Mother and/or Dad and give them hell for what happened twenty years ago. Unfortunately, they wouldn't understand what we are talking about anyway. But you cannot just hide the anger either saying, "Poor Mom, she did the best she could." The only way we can free ourselves from the anger and prevent it from affecting our present life is to try to understand what went on then. We must acknowledge the anger but realize it is inappropriate to who and where we are today.

This is the work of psychotherapy. Can seeing a psychiatrist really help? "I don't believe in all this therapy junk," one mother of two admitted. "I hated my past life, my childhood, my high school years, my single days. I want to forget it all. At last, my life is more to my liking. The *last* thing I want to do is bring back those old miseries."

Unfortunately, it is not possible to completely forget the past as if it never happened. No matter what we might think, the past has a great deal to do with what a woman feels and how a woman reacts in the present.

One does not have to be crazy to handle anger in a crazy way. So much of what goes on in our minds is unconscious. These unconscious feelings are intimately connected to earlier feelings and experiences.

Psychotherapy helps illuminate our unconscious patterns. As you continue to talk about your daily and past life, patterns are visible to both the patient and the therapist. What happens during the process is, as our destructive patterns become clear to us, almost without conscious thought, we begin to develop new healthier ways of reacting. The views of a patient and a psychiatrist will help us understand how this process works.

A Patient's View

Janet is a thirty-seven-year-old social worker. She is married and has three children.

"My mother was always afraid of my father. She is the blending-into-the-wallpaper type: shy and quiet. My mother could not bear anger. Instead, she withdrew. On Sundays, when Dad would take us out, she'd stay home and clean.

"I was Daddy's baby. I was his favorite, everyone knew it. It was always my father and I versus my mother and sister. Then, at age nine, my world fell apart. My father died. I was totally devastated. I felt like an orphan. I felt totally abandoned. I could not continue. I threatened to kill myself. I got extremely upset if my mother went out.

"So my mother took me for therapy. She could not handle it anymore. At first I thought it was just a lark—a way to get out of school early. But then I liked going. My therapist was a loving, caring man who I continued to see for three years. During my appointment, my mother met with a social worker. It 'helped us both.

"At age twenty-two, single and lonely, I went again. I saw a therapist on and off for five years. He gave me tremendous support. For the first time in my life, I had positive feelings about myself.

"My anger at my father affects my feelings towards my husband, indeed all men. I do not trust men. I feel they will never be there when you need them. With my husband, I feel I just can't depend on him because he'll probably disappoint me. And somehow, he always *does* disappoint me.

"When my first child was born, he was very sick. I relived exactly all the feelings I had when I was nine years old and my father died. There was an overwhelming sense of loss. There was that old bargaining, 'God, if you do this...'

"My anger never does go away despite all the therapy. I really don't think my disappointment with men and my anger at them will ever go away. But therapy has gotten me through the toughest times.

"Of course, as a child and for a long time, I did not know I was angry at my father. The first time I really learned the truth about my father was when I was nearly twenty-five. My therapist showed me my father's hospital records.

"My father had killed himself. As a pharmacist, he knew exactly what he was doing. He wanted to die when he took that overdose."

Psychiatrists explain that loss is a common cause of anger. Erik Erikson, in his book *Childhood and Society*, explains that one's dependence needs are determined in childhood. One of the first traits a child develops is trust. This trust is based on predictability—verbal and non-verbal reassurances. When this predictability is suddenly destroyed, the child flounders. This causes immense anger. The loss of a parent in early childhood tends to make a person more susceptible to loss throughout her life.

In Janet's case, her loss was so sudden, the anger was even greater. Dr. Russell A. Meares, M.D., in his article "On Saying Goodbye before Death," which appeared in the September 1981 *Journal of the American Medical Society*, explained that the living have a role in comforting the dying, but the dying also have a role in preparing for the well-being of the survivors. Despite illness, most dying people do say farewell in a way that lets the survivors know they have been loved and valued. But in the case of suicide, there is a deliberate refusal to make a farewell.

The survivors have questions that can never be answered. In short, suicide leaves them in turmoil. The suicide victim may have quelled his own torment but he has condemned his survivors to it forever.

Therapy can explain the reason for complex and painful feelings. The term "psychotherapy" means techniques that help a person develop insights into what may be causing her feelings and then practical ways to cope with those feelings. There is nothing mysterious or foreboding about psychotherapy. Professionals—whether psychiatrists, psychologists or therapists—are not wizards. They cannot wave a magic wand and make life's problems disappear, but psychotherapy can help us cope with deeply ingrained feelings due to long-past and unchangeable childhood events.

A Psychiatrist's View

Irma Zelig, M.D., is attending in psychiatry at Beth Israel Medical Center and Mt. Sinai Medical Center and a private psychotherapist in New York City.

"Why must we go back to our childhood when we can't

change it anyway?" we asked Dr. Zelig. She explained how childhood is indeed where it all begins—where our feelings about ourselves and our way of relating to others is established. As adults, we simply follow patterns set when we were very young.

"You can't undo what happened during your childhood but you can undo its consequences. The consequences are reflected in how you relate to others today.

"If you are not getting the results you want in a present relationship, the cause, most certainly, is in how your parents helped or didn't help you as a child to express your angry feelings. If your parents became angry at you for being angry, if they would not tolerate your anger, you may have repressed the angry feelings without even realizing it. Inevitably, you will repress anger as an adult.

"The way you act in the present is a reflection and repetition of the primary relationships in your past. These primary relationships—those with a mother and father—have molded how you feel about yourself. That self-image becomes your way of relating.

"Some people have misconceptions about therapy. They think they will suddenly understand their whole personalities based on one traumatic event. The 'Eureka, it was that Sunday when...' type of thing. Unfortunately, things are not so simple. What happens to most of us are strained interactions with a mother or father throughout our childhood. Such relationships have long-lasting effects.

"If a mother has been rejecting or ambivalent, it leads to a loss of self-esteem in the child. The child becomes more demanding because his basic demands have not been satisfied.

"If a mother was emotionally rejecting, a child will become a mistrusting adult, always looking on the negative side of things. Most people tend to blame the outside world for their difficulties. Certainly, the outside world is not blameless. You might have an extremely demanding boss, an uncompromising husband, a handicapped child. Yet the important thing is your reaction to the situation.

"In many cases, we set up situations which then make us angry. For example, a woman might be very angry at her mother-in-law. A neutral thing she does might be seen as something very offensive because of things her own mother did.

"Our childhood experiences greatly affect our marriage. For both women and men, marriage is often a subconscious struggle to resolve a relationship with our mothers that may have been troublesome. Many women say they prefer the holding and cuddling, not the genital part of sex. Essentially, this is the mothering they are craving.

"Of course, we are not really aware of why we react to situations in certain ways. This is because our real motivations are subconscious. Therapy helps us unravel and see how we distort.

"Therapy begins with today, the here and now. From now, we proceed to 'When have I experienced this before?' we begin to look back. But therapy is not an intellectual exercise. It is an emotional living through. After about two sessions, most therapists can identify many subconscious motivations. If the therapist wrote it all down and gave us her analysis, however, it would be no good whatsoever. Only by emotionally experiencing the feelings again...by minutely going over events, can we begin to unravel our self-damaging emotional patterns."

The majority of women we spoke with were aware of their feelings and their anger. However, they were practical women, fascinated by psychological talk, but unwilling emotionally and unable financially to undertake therapy without end. So I asked Dr. Zelig:

Why does a woman seek professional help? "It is not because she is crazy or has secret phobias. A woman seeks therapy because she is continually unhappy; her life is not working out as she would like. Her chronic anger usually manifests itself as depression."

How long does therapy last? "This is highly variable, but at least a few years. A lifetime of interacting cannot be changed in a few sessions. It is much like getting a college degree. It takes a long time and you must work hard. But you are not suddenly all-knowing when you are handed the diploma. You are growing and learning all along."

How many times a week is required? "Again, this is variable. People do not realize it is the healthier person who comes more often. They can take the emotional intensity."

Is therapy for everyone? "Not at all. For some people, psychotherapy is definitely counterindicated. It can be destructive. These people have built up defenses which they desperately need to survive emotionally. Others have appropriate feelings of anger. If a husband walks out or a son dies, we may feel angry at our fate. This is healthy and normal. To feel otherwise would be decidedly unhealthy. As long as the anger can be experienced and then forgotten, therapy is not needed."

Anger can be a way of maintaining a tie to our parents. Sometimes we continue to be angry that mother or father wasn't the way we, as children, would have liked. As long as we remain fixed on resentment of what they did or didn't do, as long as we can go on blaming them, we don't have to take responsibility for our own lives. The past becomes our excuse, an escape valve.

Going for professional help is never done casually. It is a step most of us try to avoid. Dr. Douglas Powell, a Harvard-trained psychologist and author of *Understanding Human Adjustment,* has stated, "Usually there are three things that prevent us from seeking help when we need it: a sense that the trouble really isn't so bad; a feeling that something simple is going to help, like will-power or just saying our prayers every night; and the fact that the craziness isn't there all the time."

Therapy can be helpful but we cannot expect it to bring us happiness. As Freud himself said, "Psychoanalysis, even when successful, can promise little more than to convert hysterical misery into common unhappiness."

While others may see few changes (they may notice we are calmer), the people in therapy usually feel a definite change. They feel less anxious, less depressed and less angry. They are more content with themselves and more contained within themselves. They have less need to prove themselves to others. Most of all, they feel a relief from ever-present tension.

One forty-three-year-old divorcee explained her feelings about therapy this way:

> "It has been the best thing I have ever done. I have found my ego again. I can smile and laugh. I'm happy to be alive every day. I don't feel that constant pressure from someone always finding fault. For a long time, I was frightened. My husband said that our marriage was all my fault and I believed him. I began to doubt my own perceptions and what I should feel. From that resulted confusion, self-doubt and a downward spiral. I was convinced I was crazy. It took years of therapy to straighten it all out.
>
> "My first therapy was disaster. I had never been before and had no idea what to expect. The psychiatrist told me I was a bitch, a conniving woman. He put me on medicine. But everything just made me worse. I wound up in a hospital.
>
> "Later I went to a woman therapist who said I was not crazy. I could relate to her, talk to her. She was very kind, gentle and supportive. She ethnically understood my background. Most of all, I always felt she was *in my corner*."

Psychotherapy can bring us an understanding of what is really making us angry. It can expose our unhealthy patterns and help us correct our harmful ways. And most importantly, it can elicit our personal strengths, enabling us to turn the page on life's adversities and go forward.

4

Anger in the Single Life

"I don't want to go out dancing and drinking. I want someone who thinks I am absolutely terrific. I want someone who knows all about me and still thinks I'm the greatest."

A thirty-one-year-old market researcher

"More than anything in the world, I want to be married. But it's not happening. I feel frustrated. I feel angry. I want something and I can't get it...."

A twenty-eight-year-old teacher

"I have no great need to run out and get married. I like

making my own decisions. I can support myself very well.
What I need and want is someone I can depend on. I want
to feel if I need him, he'll be there. When we talk, I want to
feel that things are better."

A thirty-four-year-old fabric designer

Being single has been compared to diving off the high board
for the first time as a child. It's a lot easier to appreciate when
it's over and you are laughing about it with your friends than
when it's happening and you are stranded in midair.

"The more Mr. Wrongs I meet, the more angry I become," a
thirty-eight-year-old single dancer explained. "After a while, I
say to myself, why can't I find someone. What's wrong with
me? "

Many single women seek therapy because they are intensely
unhappy without a man. They believe there is something
wrong with them. They feel devalued and inadequate. Raised
to believe that all women could look forward to love and
marriage, they feel left out and cheated.

Because so many single women we spoke with voiced confu-
sion as much as anger, we asked Dr. Iris Ascher, a New York
City psychiatrist and assistant professor of psychiatry at Albert
Einstein Medical Center, her ideas on anger in the single life.

"I'll tell you the major thing women complain about: MEN. I
see single women from ages twenty to sixty but their complaints
are very similar. They say it is very, very difficult to meet men.
And when they *are* lucky enough to find an interesting man,
they talk about the 'Tuesday night syndrome.' They find the
men they do meet are unwilling to commit themselves.

"Interestingly, all women—married women and single women
alike—almost exclusively talk to me about relationships. Even
highly successful career women talk about interpersonal relationships. But men complain much less about women. They do
not seem as deeply bothered by interpersonal things. Men talk

about career pressures, financial problems. They are extremely concerned with success at work.

"I do not think the problems of the single women are entirely psychological. There are also social factors that play a major role. There *are* more women than men. Men *do* date younger women. Men *are* less interested in permanence than women.

"In my practice, I see that men get reinvolved very quickly. In three to six months, men always find a new woman. Some don't even end one relationship before beginning a new one. They have no lapses at all. But after a relationship a woman can commonly be without a man for four years! They feel tremendous vulnerability, loneliness, sadness and rejection. They very rarely convert this to anger. It stays as loneliness, sadness and hurt. They talk about hurt and upset, not anger.

"The single women I see are definitely lonely. Even those with many interests find these don't take care of all their needs.

"What do I advise? Generally, of course I don't advise anything. I cannot change social factors. But when asked, I do stress affiliation.

"The more people you meet, the more real interests you pursue, the more active you are, the better your chance of meeting people. The larger your network and contacts, the better the odds. This means getting out of your apartment and making a large effort. Unfortunately, sometimes it just does not work out, but sometimes it does."

Society's view of the single woman just adds to the anger. "People view the single woman as a reject. No matter what I accomplish, I still don't have the status of a married woman," a thirty-two-year-old bank executive explained.

"That old stigma has not changed a bit," a thirty-four-year-old teacher said angrily. "I feel it all the time...in job interviews, in relationships with men, even in relationships with married couples. If you're divorced and thirty-five, it's okay. But if you've never been married and thirty-five, everyone concludes something is wrong."

This idea of an unspeakable flaw was echoed over and over by single men—even supposedly sophisticated, liberal-thinking men. While considering themselves a great catch, they thought of single women as losers. One young doctor said, "I'm always meeting women with children. Now I'm dating a girl who's really great. But she's thirty-four and never been married. I'll have to find our what's wrong with her."

Prejudice against "singles" is even seen within the family. A single thirty-eight-year-old advertising executive whose sister is married with two children explained, "My mother is always bragging about my sister. What really irritates me is she's always bringing her the most extravagant gifts. Of course she brings me things too. But it never evens out. She gets much more even though she really needs it less. It happens over and over."

Psychiatrists explain that such daily verbal and non-verbal messages have a profound effect on a person's mood. If one's environment is supportive and confirms a healthy sense of self-esteem, people feel good about themselves. On the other hand, if the environment provides no release, anger boils inside.

The single stigma might in fact be totally unfounded. Sociologist Jessie Bernard has a theory that in any group of older singles, the men will be comparatively the losers while the women will be actually the cream of the crop. This is because Dr. Bernard believes that American women are taught to "marry up"—to someone smarter, older, taller, richer, a man who will "take care of you." On the other hand, men are taught to "marry down"—to someone younger, weaker, and with less status whom he might "take care of." The single man, therefore, may have been so "bad" he could not find anyone "lower" while the woman may be so "great" it is difficult to find someone better who is also available.

For years, people assumed that single not only meant misfits but also misery. While recent studies do *not* show that singles suffer more depression, as traditionally assumed, being alone *is* difficult in our society. We live in a "couple culture."

"I found the uncoupling one of the worst parts of the divorce," admitted a thirty-year-old teacher. "I wanted the divorce but it knocked out all the props, all the security." Another divorced woman, forty-two years old, commented, "This town is like Noah's Ark, if you aren't part of a pair, they shut you out."

Psychologically, the hurt of being left out probably goes back to childhood. The most basic oedipal conflict involves a wish to be part of a couple. The desire for coupling begins early in childhood and continues throughout adult life.

Male-female emotional differences may also make being alone more difficult for women. A little boy is taught to accomplish things. On the other hand, a little girl is more likely to dress up and be concerned with pleasing others. The approval of others has traditionally been more important for women then men.

While society's pressures affect everyone, our own attitude is probably the most important happiness factor. A fifty-year-old single woman, who has been living with a married man for several years, remarked, "I've never wanted to get married. I like being my own master. I don't need an appendage: I don't have to go two by two. I like being able to do what I want when I like. Because it's never been a goal for me, I don't feel disappointed or angry. Many women feel marriage is their due, they feel they are missing something. From the marriages I've seen, I don't think I'm missing a thing! I don't feel my being is incomplete."

When asked about her current love affair, she happily remarked, "Oh, I don't want to marry him. He has a wife; I'm the girlfriend! It's a perfect situation. I can have my freedom and him too."

While marriage may or may not be a goal, "dating" is awkward at best; the dating situation makes it difficult to really know a man. "Sometimes I meet a new man and it's total nervousness. I feel like screaming at him, 'Why are you acting like this?' " a twenty-three-year-old stenciling artist explained. "I start to think it's me. I can't really talk to anyone. Then, I get angry and confused."

Despite these common feelings, most women do eventually fall in love. Why there is a spark with one man and absolutely nothing with another is still a mystery. Some fascinating findings suggest however it probably has more to do with "us" than "him."

Everyone develops strong attachments (yes, love) for their self-made images of their mate. They are more in love with their mental picture than with the real person.

People who use these mental frames are neither dishonest, nor sick, nor excessively insecure. We all do it. Sociologists believe such images are even essential to bringing people together.

While human beings have a tremendous capacity for adoring fantasy figures (perhaps the reason cult figures and dead heroes are so beloved), the poignant truth is most people have more trouble loving real human beings.

Unfortunately, most of us judge and choose one another based on superficial factors. This is neither fair (most of these factors are beyond our control; they are inborn) nor wise.

The real truth is that one of the first attractions for a man is a woman's breasts. "In high school the most popular girls were always the ones with big breasts," a thirty-five-year-old divorcée explained. "Pretty didn't matter, breasts were everything. Now I'm divorced and you know what? It's exactly the same. Breasts bring the men."

Because breasts are so important, breast development at either end of the development spectrum will cause tremendous anger. A girl whose breasts develop far ahead of her peers may feel isolated and angry. The late-blooming adolescent also perceives herself as different and this may become a focus of low self-esteem and anger.

Generally liking one's breasts means a young girl likes herself and feels worthwhile. Sheila Klefarour, M.D., Assistant Clinical Professor of Psychiatry at New York Medical College, Valhalla, has stated, "A young girl who is satisfied with her breasts is apt to have a less troubled adolescence than one who has conflicts about breast development."

While several years ago large breasts were so prized that a Dutch sociologist dubbed America "the udder society," today large breasts are less envied. However, unhappiness with one's breasts can continue long after styles change. A twenty-seven-year-old writer admitted, "I've always been unhappy with my breasts. When I was growing up, I always envied girls with big breasts. In college, I wore one of those padded bras and I was embarrassed if a guy tried to dance close. I thought he could tell. Now, I'm more pleased with my breasts. But when sex in my marriage declines for a while, I often wonder, 'Would it be better if I had bigger breasts?' "

In her famous essay "A Few Words about Breasts," Nora Ephron, describing many common insecurities and anger concerning breast size, writes:

"Now that I am grown-up enough to understand that most of my feelings have very little to do with the reality of my shape, I am nonetheless obsessed by breasts. I cannot help it. I grew up in the terrible Fifties—with rigid stereotypical sex roles, the insistence that men be men and dress like men and women be women and dress like women, the intolerance of androgyny— and I cannot shake it, cannot shake my feelings of inadequacy.... Here I am, stuck with the psychological remains of it all, stuck with my own peculiar version of breast worship....

Well, what can I tell you? If I had had them I would have been a completely different person, I honestly believe that."

Other superficial factors, such as beauty, play a large factor in single life. Some fascinating studies by Dr. Ellen Bersheid, professor of psychology at the University of Minnesota, show that being pretty is often the reason women are liked.

Her studies show that newborn infants who were independently rated as attractive were held, cuddled, and kissed more than unattractive babies. Another study found that nursery school children who were rated by adults as physically attractive were found to be more popular with their school friends.

Still another University of Minnesota study has shown that college students paired as dates at a computer dance preferred others who were physically attractive; the partners' intelligence, social skills, and personality had little to do with the students' reaction to their dates. And contrary to expectation, college students who agreed to complete five dates revealed that, as the number of dates increased, attractiveness became a *more* important factor in determining if the partner was liked.

As Americans, we want to believe that all people are born equal, with an equal chance for a happy life. But it simply is not so. The most important factors determining a person's success are genetically determined; appearance, intelligence, sex and height. Because these factors are beyond our control, their importance can cause intense anger.

While dating is often based on superficial factors, it is nonetheless tremendously important because dating selection ultimately determines our mate selection. Choosing a suitable mate may, indeed, be the secret of marital happiness since it is the dynamics of an interaction, more than individual traits, that cause conflict.

When asked her advice for a successful marriage, Helen Singer Kaplan, M.D., Ph.D., director of the Helen Kaplan Institute for the Evaluation and Treatment of Sexual Disorders in New York City, advised, "Choose the right partner! With the wrong partner, no matter how hard you work, the marriage is not likely to succeed."

Some women seem to have an uncanny knack for always choosing unsuitable men. They get into destructive relationships, are disappointed when they don't work out, but then go right back to the old pattern.

Freud explains the magnetic power of such destructive relationships as "repetition compulsion." This centers around an unconscious compulsion to try to make the bad mother we feel we had into the good one we always wanted. Repetition is due to an inability to accept that we failed with our mother. It is the subconscious feeling that we are going to prove, at last, things will be different. When things are not different and again we fail, anger—unexpressed anger turned inward—is almost always the result.

After extensive research, psychiatrists have concluded that the following guidelines make for the best combinations:

SEE EACH OTHER SIMILARLY.

Psychiatrists call the *self-concept validation.* They say it is one of the most important factors in a satisfactory relationship. For example, if a man thinks he has a sense of humor, it helps if his wife thinks he has a sense of humor. Interestingly, this congruence is important for our negative as well as positive traits. For example, if a woman thinks that she has no talent whatsoever for math, there will be greater harmony in the relationship if the husband thinks she has no talent for math.

CHOOSE A DOMINANT OR EQUAL MATE.

Despite women's liberation, studies have shown that the highest level of marital satisfaction is found in husband-dominant marriages, the next highest in equalitarian marriages and the lowest in wife-dominant structures. (In wife-dominant structures, it is usually the wife who is miserable.)

BE AWARE OF BIRTH ORDER.

A fascinating 1974 Israeli study entitled, "Birth Order and Marital Bliss," showed that a first-born husband and a later-born wife make for the happiest couple. The next happiest in order are: (2) a later-born husband with a first-born wife, (3) a middle-born husband or middle-born wife married to any other, (4) an only child married with a first-born, (5) a first-born husband married to a first-born wife, (6) a later-born husband and a later-born wife and, finally, (7) an only child married to another only child. So if you are both only children, think about things carefully!

CHOOSE SOMEONE INTELLECTUALLY SIMILAR BUT EMOTIONALLY COMPLEMENTARY.

A recent 1977 study showed that marital satisfaction is optimal when the partner's intellectual values are similar and their emotional characteristics are complementary.

While "like attracts like" in education, religion and race, opposites attract in emotional areas. A dominant person is more likely to be attracted to a submissive person than to another dominant person.

It is difficult to date, even casually, without becoming at least somewhat involved. When a relationship ends, there is always hurt. A twenty-three-year-old salesgirl told about a recent parting:

"I was going out with a guy for a few weeks. One evening, he said, 'I think we ought to have a talk.' When he said that, my heart just went into my stomach. He said, 'I don't think you are the one for me.' Initially, it hurt me. It really hurt a lot. Then I thought about it. He was right. I wasn't the girl for him. Even though I knew it, to hear him say it was hurtful."

A twenty-nine-year-old computer saleswoman who had just married two months ago told how she handled the ending of relationships:

"After I broke up with someone, I would go through a lot of self-destruction. I'd change my life style drastically. I'd go out indiscriminately, have sex with anyone. I was an easy mark, I would go to bars alone and drink and inevitably end up with some guy. I would have sex with these guys and get rid of them in the morning. I actually hate going to bars, so that was something I did in times of rejection and anger mainly because I hated myself. I'd take a walk on the wild side for a while.

"I think it was a way of trying to regain the upper hand. After about a month, I'd be normal again. Inevitably, I'd go on a diet. I could never control my eating if I was in a terrible mood. These times were tough but I'd regain tremendous strength from going through them."

Breaking up is almost never a mutual decision. One person is always more emotionally involved and therefore hurt more deeply. The hurt is due to bruised ego, change of habit, and true sorrow of missing someone you loved. Such hurt can only be healed with time. It can take as long as three or four years, depending on the length of the relationship; for a short affair, the typical recovery is six months to a year. The hurt is compounded when a woman deeply desires permanence and it does not happen. A thirty-eight-year-old teacher confessed:

"I don't know if I am more bored or more furious inside. I'm just fed up with dating. How much dating can one tolerate? I've been dating for twenty years!

"What I want is something permanent. The impermanence of dating is just awful. It's hard to enjoy a date for what it is. It's hard to look at it as just an enjoyable evening. I'm constantly projecting six months, a year down the road. I'm always thinking about the potential for a permanent relationship in this date. Now I am more sure of my wants and needs. But when things don't work out, I am still devastated. I've had enough rejections."

How you handle anger in a dating relationship depends on your self-confidence. All of us are insecure and need to feel loved. But excessive dependency is usually related to poor self-esteem. The lower a person's self-esteem, the more terrified she is of anger, fearing rejection.

Lessening anger is a process. Each incident is a small step towards more risk-taking, greater confidence and, most of all, self-appreciation.

So many single women seemed angrier at other women than at men, we felt this anger could not be overlooked. "There is fierce competition among women," a thirty-eight-year-old advertising sales executive commented. "I remember I wanted to be my Dad's favorite over my sister. I remember competition from the age of two or three for my Dad. There was competition with my sister and with my Mom. And it has not stopped yet.

"Women view other women as a threat. All the women's liberation and sister business is just lip service. It works only as long as it does not threaten them. As a single attractive woman, I am always seen as a threat. I have some very close married friends. Nothing has ever been said but I can feel they would just assume I should not come in contact with their husbands. I feel a lot of anger at that situation. It really limits me. And it is unfair because I'm *not* after their husbands."

While we cannot control others—whether a boyfriend loves and cares about us or not—we are in absolute control of our anger: Each of us is in charge of what we feel and capable of changing it. Here are some approaches other single women and mental health experts say are helpful.

OLD WAY: WHEN ANGRY, WE PUT OURSELVES DOWN AND BLAME OURSELVES.

NEW APPROACH: WE KNOW THAT BEING HURT WILL NOT KILL US.

"Anger is a luxury," a twenty-one-year-old photographer told us. "It means you're not taking any blame yourself. I'm still too insecure for that. I still feel I'm to blame most of the time when things don't work out. At college, when I broke up with someone I really cared about I was so angry. I was angry at him. I was angry at life. I was angry at God for making it like that. Most of all, I was angry at myself. I kept going over incidents in my mind. If only I had been cooler, less honest, smarter, more attractive. It went on and on."

Women, more than men, tend to blame themselves when a dating relationship does not succeed. Therapists say that even when talking about a positive trait, many women will cancel it out with a negative. Sally Snullen, a thirty-two-year-old twice divorced mother of two, was very typical. She explained, "People say I am warm and friendly but maybe I'm too friendly. I don't pick my friends carefully enough."

One of the reasons we become so hurt and angry is we feel the relationship *should* work. We blame ourselves. We do anything to hold on to a relationship fearing a breakup would destroy us. The truth is that most dating relationships do not work out. Breakups are more common than permanence. We all can and do survive the loss of love. Such disappointment is *not* a personal failure; it is an event which happens to most people several times. It does not mean that we, as individuals, need a psychiatrist. It does not mean that something is wrong with us. Realizing this will help you cope with a difficult period more realistically.

OLD WAY: I LOVE JOHN BUT HE DOESN'T *REALLY* LOVE ME. HE COULD WALK OUT TOMORROW AND IT WOULDN'T EVEN BOTHER HIM.

NEW APPROACH: I UNDERSTAND THAT INDIVID-UAL CAPACITIES FOR LOVING VARY GREATLY.

The ancient lovers' quarrel over who loves whom the most often begins during dating and can last a lifetime. It is based on the fact that the person who loves the most is more vulnerable and therefore insecure. People rarely realize it but in *every* relationship one partner is more in love than the other. This is natural. It may fluctuate from time to time or there may be permanent differences. Individual capacities for loving vary. When these disparities are seen as facts of life rather than personal hurts, less anger will result.

OLD WAY: I FELT IF HE WANTED TO DANCE WITH ME HE WOULD ASK ME.

NEW APPROACH: IF I SEE A GUY I LIKE, I ALWAYS SMILE, ACT VERY FRIENDLY AND ASK HIM IF HE WOULD LIKE TO DANCE.

A more aggressive approach by women today does not only show a changing society; it shows greater self-confidence. A black divorced mother of one who loves disco dancing explained, "I'm very overweight. I used to feel terrible if no one asked me to dance. I'd sit and wait. Sometimes all I did was wait. But now I feel that's for the birds. I'll come up with some silly excuse. I'll say, 'Why are you sitting all by yourself when you could be dancing with me?' Or sometimes just, 'May I join you?' It sounds corny but it usually works. If it doesn't, I'll ask someone else. Almost always, I get a partner for the night that way."

OLD WAY: SEX MEANS "DOING WHAT COMES NATURALLY."

NEW APPROACH: SEXUAL HONESTY AT THE BEGINNING OF A RELATIONSHIP CAN ENHANCE SATISFACTION AND REDUCE FRUSTRATION AND PROBLEMS LATER ON.

Relying on "doing what comes naturally" is difficult because what comes naturally in sexual situations is all sorts of worry: worry about sufficient attractiveness; about how to persuade a partner to become cooperative; about being rejected; about sexual incompetence; about being too sophisticated or too naive; about fulfilling sexual expectations.

Faking in sex often begins, as so many hidden intimate conflicts do, during dating. New sex mates are so eager to please and to be experienced as pleasing, they often are sexually deceptive.

The most common form of sexual deception is the faking of orgasms. Women, obviously, can get away with faking easier than a man. A man cannot fake sperm ejaculations but his sex-faking can consist of such techniques as exaggerating passion, escalating pelvic thrust to imitate orgasm, withdrawing and pretending that he feared impregnation and therefore preferred not to come "inside of you."

The problem is that couples establish a repertoire of sexual routines during courtship. If these routines turn out to have been based on fakery rather than genuine likes and dislikes, a situation may be perpetuated which is very difficult to break without great harm.

Contrary to myth, variety is not always the answer. Most people find sex variety stimulating in fantasy but not reality. Most couples—even dating couples—establish a sexual routine. Suggestions given in the aura of romance—for example, "I love it when you..." will help establish a satisfying sex pattern.

OLD WAY: I'M TRYING TO MEET "MR. RIGHT."
NEW APPROACH: THERE IS A PLACE FOR DIFFERENT RELATIONSHIPS AS LONG AS I KNOW WHERE I STAND.

"Knowing where you stand in a love relationship is crucial to prevent hurt and anger," a forty-four-year-old woman who has been legally separated for two years explained. "Understanding is the key to everything. I'll date a man I would never marry. I put him in a mental area and know he could never enter a deeper sphere. I find hurt only comes if you're fooled. Men will sometimes try to use you, to take advantage of you. They will say dishonest things, try to get new business contacts, or try to get your money. If you know from the beginning what to expect, I think you can handle almost anything."

While dating can cause tremendous anger, just blurting out our anger does not resolve it. Bringing things into the open does not automatically make them better. In fact, talking can sometimes make people even angrier.

Jennifer, a single thirty-nine-year-old advertising executive saleswoman, told us, "I had a terrible fight with my boyfriend last night. He was very mean to me; he really hit below the belt. I think that's *it*. I find in dating, when there is a bad fight, it is almost never discussed, it just ends the relationship."

To prevent a disastrous and perhaps unnecessary break-up, it may be useful to ask questions. Questions rather than declarative statements tend to cool the emotional fires and prevent honest confusion and misunderstanding.

Being single is emotionally difficult. One woman confessed, "My whole being was so occupied with my singleness, I found it difficult—no, impossible—to put my energies to other things. However, being single teaches women they must stand on their own two feet. Achieving a sense of self-worth and financial self-sufficiency are perhaps the best lessons in coping with life's stresses."

5

Sex: The Third Party in Bed

66**W**hen I don't express my anger out of bed, it often shows up in bed," Jane Rolling, a thirty-five-year-old advertising executive, married for the second time, explained. "I remember one incident that was so typical. Ed had given me a terrible time all day and I hadn't said anything. In the morning, he reached his hand under my nightgown and touched my clitoris. I felt total rage. I screamed, 'Don't you dare do that.' My pent-up anger just erupted uncontrollably.

"Another time, I had also been angry but kept it in. When Ed wanted sex, all I could think about was getting this over with. He stuck his finger first into my vagina and then stuck the same finger into my mouth. I bit his finger so hard, he went into a total rage. His anger was a rejection response. But my anger was the accumulation of a lot of angers. I was also angry at myself for not saying right away, 'I'm not in the mood.' I should never have let sex take place. I was insanely repulsed and angry. Honestly, I don't think he meant it as a degrading act; he found it stimulating. Within a few seconds it was over. We both went back to bed—one on each side, of course—with no words spoken. But it was an incident I'll never forget."

One woman, a housewife and mother of three, told us she was never really sexually relaxed. "When Jack and I get into bed there's always a strain. I'm nervous because I'm never sure how things will be. Should I initiate things or will Jack feel pressured? Will it be okay this time? These things are always on my mind. Often, Jack just climbs into his side of the bed, turns his back towards me and goes to sleep. That way we don't confront the problem but I still feel rejected, hurt and, yes, angry."

A thirty-two-year-old single book editor commented:

"I have never used sex as a weapon. And other women I know are the same. It's the men who withhold sex as a punishment. For example, I like to take showers with my boyfriends. One time when this guy I really liked came home, I said, in a cute way, 'I waited till you came home to take a shower.' Rather than picking up on it, he snapped at me. He acted angry at me. I'm much more careful now. In my experience, it's the men who are saying no, never the women."

For both sexes, honest (but sometimes secret) feelings about a partner are reflected in how we feel and act sexually. When anger is at the root of our feelings, sexual problems often result. These problems can limit sexual contact, thus creating more problems.

"Frank talk about the way someone behaved at a dinner party is easier than talking about someone's insensitivity to physical and emotional needs in bed," a forty-year-old divorcée said. "What usually happens to me is I feel some irritation and because it is not addressed, sexually there is a withdrawal of feeling. 'I just don't feel like it tonight,' I'll say, or 'I'm tired,' but in my heart I know my lack of desire is almost always due to anger."

Anger is likely to accumulate in sexual matters because it is very difficult for most people to discuss sex honestly. While talking openly is always recommended, few people actually do it. Sometimes even talking does not help, as my friend Sally, a thirty-five-year-old single teacher, explained:

"I had a partner who insisted on doing things the same way each and every time. In particular, it would help him reach a climax if I touched my vagina and clitoris. His ability was dependent on me doing something to myself. This angered me since I didn't always feel like doing that. If I didn't, I felt I was letting him down. If I did it but I hated doing it, I felt deceitful. Finally, I exploded. I said, 'I don't want to.' I would like to say that he understood but he didn't. I think it ended the relationship. So many times I see tremendous male selfishness in bed. They want sex their way and that's it."

Janice Walters, a forty-year-old divorced woman, described her long relationship with a man she almost married this way:

"This man was very, very important to me. We went together for five years. During sex, he always displayed a basic selfishness. He concentrated on his own erotic stimulation. He was lost in his own erotic fantasies and seemed only concerned with what was pleasing to him. He never tried to find out the parallels for me. His way of lovemaking had its own pleasures for me. But the fact that there was no intent whatsoever to find out what would be pleasing to me was a source of great anger.

"What happened? After months of wanting to talk about it but being afraid to bring the topic up, afraid he would leave, afraid I would lose him, I finally did say something. I just asked him if he would hold me and caress me. I just wanted to be touched more. I felt this was a very mild comment. It was couched between all sorts of phrases about how much he meant to me and how much and deeply I cared for him. As much as I'd like to report this brought us closer, what in fact happened was, he abruptly jumped out of bed, started to get dressed shouting, 'I am the way I am. I will not take instruction. You take the whole package or you don't take it at all.' So I did put up with things for another three months. But the affair ended."

Unfortunately, Sally and Janice's experiences are not unusual. When sexual techniques show self-centeredness, anger is inevitable.

"My husband feels he's not a good lover technically," Cheryl, a forty-nine-year-old mother of one, explained. "I know I should be understanding, but instead of making an effort, he just lies there and lets me do things to him. He doesn't make the slightest effort to do anything to give me pleasure. It makes me furious. Somehow he feels by getting hard and putting it in, he's done everything required. I think he should put himself out a little. But he does absolutely nothing."

A thirty-eight-year-old single secretary agreed, saying, "I meet a lot of men who don't like oral sex. That makes me angry. They don't like putting their tongue inside a woman. But they just love it when a woman performs oral sex. They like to receive pleasure but they really can't be bothered to give it."

While there has been a great emphasis on sexual techniques, studies have shown that by far the most important factor in sexual satisfaction is not technique but frequency. The "quantity not quality" theory has just been substantiated again by the latest studies of Dr. Ellen Frank at the University of Pittsburgh's Department of Psychiatry. She studied one hundred "happily" married couples. What she found was that these couples all had sexual problems—even dysfunctions, including premature ejaculation, too little foreplay, lack of tenderness after lovemaking and so on. The one variable about sex that *did* affect happiness however was frequency. The "happy" couples did not have sex skillfully; they just had sex *a lot!*

Dr. Alan J. Wahreh, Associate Professor of Obstetrics and Gynecology at the University of Connecticut School of Medicine, agrees. "Twenty years of marriage counseling research has shown without doubt that the most important sexual factor in marital happiness is frequency." In *Sexual Behavior in the Seventies*, Morton Hunt gives data showing that close couples have sex fifty percent more frequently than distant couples!

Besides frequency, probably the most common woman's sexual complaint is inadequate foreplay. Over and over, women told us, men were sexually in too much of a hurry; they were too rough and perfunctory. A forty-year-old woman explained:

"I like things slow. I'm slow in everything—eating, talking, even walking. I like to savor things. I'm the same with sex. But my husband is like a train racing out of control during sex. It leaves me unsatisfied and it makes me angry."

A thirty-year-old single jewelry designer commented:

"I guess I'm getting too used to my vibrator. It seems men are always impatient or too turned on. If a man's penis is inside me and he's stimulating me manually, he's always in such a hurry. It takes me time to have an orgasm. I have to be able to relax. But men don't have that much self-control or maybe they don't really care. Sometimes it's all over when I am just getting started."

Long before Masters and Johnson, it was known that the

main tension between the sexes during copulation was the difference in pace. While men climax within a few minutes, women generally need more time to become aroused. It takes an experienced orgasmic woman ten to twenty minutes to climax once sexual stimulation has begun (the actual intercourse takes two to five minutes).

Foreplay creates a feeling of being loved that brings sexual arousal. For this to happen however foreplay needs to be relaxed and unhurried. When foreplay lasts twenty minutes or more, the woman is more likely to have orgasm, studies say, than when it lasts less than twenty minutes. Furthermore, the longer the penile intromission, the greater the chance for female orgasm.

All women do not have the same foreplay needs; and a woman may need foreplay one time but not the next. Variations in arousal patterns are related to feelings or thoughts at a given time, as well as hormonal changes during the menstrual cycle.

But all women do have a very basic need to be held and touched. Indeed, one researcher has even suggested that women become involved in casual sex due to a deep need to be touched rather than a feeling of loneliness, insecurity or even sexual desire.

While foreplay problems are common in women, the time immediately after sex also causes anger. Once physical ejaculation is enjoyed, a man is usually quiet, satisfied and unresponsive. In women, however, orgasm may lead to a strong and intense desire for repetition. An abrupt turning away by a man can leave a woman feeling unappreciated, unloved and angry.

Whether to have sex or not brings confusion to women of all ages and sexual experience who are just dating. Many times, a woman will become involved early in a sexual relationship because she desperately wants to have a relationship. In becoming sexually involved, she feels she will win approval, security and love. Yet, often the results are not as she hoped as Jennifer Lee, a twenty-year-old college sophomore, told us,

> "I'd like to have a real relationship but at college you always have to sleep with a guy by the third date. And there is never any commitment. If you don't sleep with them, you are out. Even if you do, you are out in a few weeks anyway.
>
> "Recently a guy I really liked and had been sleeping with broke up with me. I was devastated. I almost dropped out of college. But he went right merrily along showing his manhood. I think I was more like part of a proud collection he had than a relationship. It really hurt me and infuriated me that I got myself in such a situation."

Today, many men view sex as purely a physical act and one they are "owed" after an evening out. This misguided expectation leads to frustration and anger in both men and women. A twenty-three-year-old shipping company administrative assistant explained:

> "I'll never forget one evening. I was invited to dinner and the theater by a man I met at a party. We had a really nice time. We went to dinner after the theater and were getting ready to go home. In the car, he turned to me and said, 'Well, are you ready to go to my place?' I said no in the nicest way. In the nastiest tone, he said, 'Get out of the car. Just get out.' And then he called me a terrible name. I felt enraged. The whole evening had all been just a calculated move. When I said no, he was furious. He barely stopped the car. I was afraid he'd run me over. Whenever I went out, there was always the question of sex. Sex always made or broke the relationship."

Mary Sams, Ph.D., a psychologist and family therapist, told us, "Because now it's okay to have sex outside marriage, many women feel obligated to say yes. Just yesterday, an attractive, intelligent divorcée explained a one-night stand by telling me, 'It was easier to sleep with him than fight with him.' And this attitude is not unusual."

With the easing of sexual standards, men are asking more— more casual sex, more extramarital affairs, more sexual excitement. Women are confused by these demands. This confusion leads to tremendous anger.

"Sex means nothing," one thirty-eight-year-old divorcée commented. "I got married in 1965 with all its morals, ethics and social techniques. Everyone believed in sex for love, sex for communication. In 1982, when I got divorced, everything had changed. Today sex has little to do with anything. It is just a social amenity like a cup of coffee after a show. I find it absolutely overwhelming."

Dealing with adult sexual needs just adds to the difficulty. A forty-five-year-old divorcée who had been married for 15 years explained, "I am a sexual woman with adult sexual needs. But when a guy turns to me after an evening in bed and says, 'Thanks honey, here take a taxi,' it's still demeaning. For common politeness I think he should see me to the door. I get angry. I feel helpless. But what can I do?"

When sex is used mainly as a physical release, the woman usually ends up feeling exploited and used. Her resentment can destroy the closeness intimacy brings, leaving only coldness, distance and anger.

While there is unquestionably more sexual activity among unmarried people today, is all this sexual activity bringing more intimacy? While lawyers like to claim that two people who climb into bed together are being intimate, the fact is both men and women can enjoy sex without any intimacy whatsoever. Increasingly this seems to be the pattern. As a twenty-seven-year-old lingerie designer, echoing the thoughts of many single women we interviewed, put it, "Most men want sex but they don't really want to hear your inner feelings. Somehow it makes them uncomfortable. They feel responsible. They feel they are somehow being pressured to tell you their deepest thoughts and they don't want to. The men I meet seem really afraid of hurt."

Whereas it was once thought marriage answered our sexual problems, today we know that marriage can also cause many sexual angers, especially in women. Interestingly, the association between pleasurable sex and marital closeness is considerably stronger for women than men. While years ago, the most sexually frustrated marital partner tended to be the husband, today it is the wife who generally suffers most.

"What are the most frequent sexual complaints in married women?" we asked Sheila Jackman, Ph.D., a psychologist and co-director of the Division of Human Sexuality at Albert Einstein College of Medicine in New York City. She explained:

"Many women are frustrated in marital sex because they feel it is not the way it is supposed to be or the way they heard it was supposed to be. In many cases, women are angry at their husbands and find it impossible to put this aside in the bedroom. 'How can I just forget and make love?' they will ask.

"A very common problem is poor communication. They will be talking but they do not understand each other. Sometimes the fact that they are talking even adds to the frustration. 'He doesn't understand, he'll never understand,' they will say. In the sexual area, they have great difficulty explaining pleasures without sounding like a traffic cop. In our sex therapy programs, we give detailed non-demand exercises which are so carefully delineated couples can't get into trouble. We also see many women who, although married, have never been sexual. Through therapy, we try to teach these women to let go in their bodies—to stop listening to all the intellectual noise in their head—and allow their bodies to release some of their pent-up anger.

" 'I don't turn him on anymore,' is a frequent feeling among married women. Sometimes sex becomes an obligation. When this happens, a woman certainly knows it and she feels tremendous hurt and anger. This anger is usually self-directed. Women, even more then men, tend to blame themselves. 'I'm not attractive enough, I'm not sexy enough,' are common feelings."

Even in marriage, there is a shyness and fear of rejection in sex. "Does he want me?" "Why do I always have to do the asking?" "Why doesn't he ever initiate sex?" "You seem interested in that other woman. Are you wishing I was she?" These questions—"my doubting questions," was how one woman described them—affect our sexual receptiveness. Many times, sex is tentatively initiated basically because a woman does not know these answers and is afraid of rejection.

Timing desire can be a tricky matter and, if not handled with consideration, this can lead to a great deal of anger. All of us experience periods of differing desire—peak times and periods of reduced desire. Sex researchers say women feel most passionate when they are least fertile. Out of 571 women interviewed in one section of the Hite Report, 320 said they craved sex most before and during their periods. Kinsey also found nine out of ten women prefer sex just before their periods.

Because marriage *does* mean a certain sexual routine, are boredom and dissatisfaction inevitable? Despite what many people think, studies do not actually show this. Indeed, over the first five years of marriage, the sexual responsiveness of the wife actually tends to increase when the marriage is a good one. One woman, married for eight years, remarked, "With us, sex is always the same. But I like it always the same. It's comfortable. It feels good and I like it that way."

"Feelings of sexual fulfillment are not only possible in marriage but more possible than in a superficial relationship," Dr. Jackman pointed out. "Fulfillment is not just orgasm. It is, first and foremost, intimacy. It is a feeling that it's okay for me to be me—with all my good parts and all my faults. It's a feeling of complete acceptance for who we are. Fulfillment does not mean constant sex. It means that the down aspects of a relationship where there is a loss of interest can be included in the relationship."

"Fulfillment," Dr. Jackman added, "is not just being there for a man. If all you care about is satisfying his needs, you won't really feel fulfilled. You must be there for him and for yourself at the same time." She explained, "I am drawing a figure eight. That's fulfillment—a flowing dancing figure that allows communication both sexual and personal to flow unrestrained."

Almost always, sexual functioning is interrelated with a person's emotional, physical, marital and family adjustments. Recent studies indicate that a much smaller percentage of people than originally thought have straightforward sex performance problems.

To deal with this complex set of interrelationships, sex therapy is sometimes recommended. How such therapy works varies greatly depending upon the person, the therapist and the difficulties. Sometimes sex therapy involves sensate focusing techniques. These teach couples to caress each other gently in a mutual non-demanding, pleasuring way. Often warm lotions or powders which give the skin a smooth, silky feeling are recommended. Couples are instructed to caress slowly and gently and to give the breasts and genitals no more attention than the rest of the body. (Intercourse is banned during these exercises.) One purpose is to give couples techniques they may want to include in foreplay. Some typical instructions are given below.

"I'd like you both to get ready for bed—to take your clothes off, shower, and relax. I want you (the woman) to lie on your belly. Then you (the man) caress her back as gently and sensitively as you can. Move your hands very slowly. Begin at the back of her neck, caress her ears, and work your way down to her buttocks, legs and feet. Use your hands and/or lips. Concentrate only on how it feels to touch her body and her skin.

"In the meantime, I want you (the woman) to focus your attention on the sensations you feel when he caresses you. Try not to let your mind wander. Don't think about anything else, don't worry about whether he's getting tired, or whether he is enjoying it or anything. Be 'selfish' and just concentrate on your own sensations; let yourself feel everything. Communicate with him. But don't talk too much or it will interfere with your responses—and his. Let him know where you want to be touched and how and where his caresses feel especially good and let him know if his touch is too light or too heavy, or if he is going too fast. Try to identify those areas of your body that are especially sensitive or responsive."

To find out more about sex therapy programs, we visited the Human Sexuality Program at Mt. Sinai Medical Center in New York City. Dr. Patricia Schreiner-Engel, a psychologist and Assistant Director of the program, answered our questions.

NOTE: For an appropriate sex therapy clinic (you must be wary since anyone can hang out a shingle and call himself a sex therapist), it is best to get a referral from your physician. Those clinics affiliated with hospitals and medical schools are generally the most reputable. Most clinics treat both couples and singles although some treat only married couples.

What actually goes on in a sex therapy clinic?
"Of course, this is the *first* thing people wonder. The fact is 'nothing' goes on in the clinic. It is all talk. If I ask a couple or individual to try a new technique, they go home and do it in the privacy of their bedroom. In the clinic, there is no performance

nor demonstrations. (Both the American Psychiatric Association and the American Psychological Association have explicit guidelines against patient-therapist sex or nudity in their code of ethics.) I will explain as clearly as possible what I'd like them to do, I may draw, show pictures, videotapes or filmstrips, if necessary.

"They will come back the following week and tell me how things went. I am interested in how they interpreted my instructions and their honest intimate feelings. Like all psychotherapy, things then progress through communication."

Who comes for sex therapy?

"Our program treats between 150 and 200 patients a year. We see both couples and individuals. It is about evenly divided between men and women.

"Interestingly, it is not always the sexually dysfunctional person who initiates the therapy, although it may be. It is the person most distressed by the difficulty who will seek help."

What age and economic groups are represented?

"It runs the total gamut. Based on legal issues, we can only treat adults over the age of consent (age eighteen). On the other end, the oldest couple we've treated was close to eighty. I am now seeing a couple in their seventies and this is not unusual.

"If I had to pick one age, I'd say for women it's the thirties. It seems their adaptive ways have worked for a while but now things are not going as well. They are not getting what they expected from their intimate relationships.

"We treat all economic groups—from the poorest to professionals and even some of the jet set."

How are patients referred to the clinic?

"There are three main sources: referrals from physicians and other hospitals, recommendations from former patients, and media coverage of our program. However, we do no advertising or organized public relations."

What does sex therapy cost?
"We charge on a sliding scale depending upon ability to pay. Charges range from eight dollars to sixty dollars a session. Private patients pay considerably more per session."

How long does sex therapy take?
"This varies tremendously, it is like asking how long does it take to learn to play the piano. It varies enormously. Certainly a person who is highly motivated and works at it can have success more quickly. The length of therapy also depends on the complexity of the problem. For simple sexual performance problems, therapy can sometimes be completed in eight to ten sessions. Sessions are once a week."

"Sometimes the therapy can take longer working with the couple together; sometimes this joint effort enables treatment to move much more quickly. It all depends on the people and their difficulties."

What are the goals of sex therapy?
"Specific goals are established by the patient in conjunction with the therapist. I will tell a patient if their goals are realistic but they are the ones to state their own priorities."

Is anger the cause of most sex problems today?
"Anger is not really a cause. Anger is a secondary feeling. It is the result of hurt and pain. Human beings cannot tolerate hurt very long, because these feelings go to their most inner being, their deepest feelings about ourselves. Because hurt is so painful, we convert it to anger. This anger then affects our interactions with others, including our sexual interactions."

Is anger in sex an easily treated problem?

"Anger is one of the most complex problems we encounter. We must understand the anger: what is it about, who is it directed at, how long has it been going on and what is the person's past adjustment to these feelings.

"The more recent the origin of the anger—some people's angers can go back to childhood, even infancy—the easier it is to treat. We try to explore whether the anger is just due to a current relationship or if it is more complex.

"Anger binds people behind a wall of armor and often renders them insensitive to their own feelings of pleasure, their sexual feelings as well as their partner's feelings. Unresolved anger can keep us from functioning successfully in many areas of life, including sex."

What is a common cause of sex anger in women?

"One of the things we see very frequently is that women are not being pleasured by their partners in ways that are conducive to a woman's becoming sexually aroused enough to achieve orgasm. This is very frustrating and eventually anger-inducing for a woman."

How is such anger treated in sex therapy?

"Of course, this again depends entirely on the two people. We try to steer women away from sounding demanding or condemning. We suggest she talk about herself, her own feelings. We try to get her to use 'I' language. This is the least threatening to a partner. We suggest she ask what he likes. This may become a model and lead him to ask what she likes.

"Many times, a woman thinks she has explained her feelings but the real message has never gotten delivered. In therapy, people come to a third party to bridge this communication gap."

Are there other common sexual angers in women?

"Many women feel they must perform on demand. Many are acutely embarrassed about sexual matters and have been confused by female sexual myths. For example, they feel they should be multiorgasmic. But medical studies show only thirty percent of all women have this capability. They feel orgasm should be achieved simultaneously. Sexual research, however, shows that in most cases this does not happen. Feeling forced to 'make' it happen or 'fake' that it happened only causes hidden anger."

Can a woman therapist be requested?

"Of course. But this is not done as much as you might think. Sometimes a woman with little sexual knowledge will feel more comfortable speaking with another woman. Sometimes it serves as a good role model. But after an initial session, a woman will probably feel at ease with the therapist regardless of his or her sex."

What is the program's success rate?

"Statistics are again difficult. What are the standards for success? How complex were the original problems? In cases of straightforward sexual dysfunction, non-physically-based, I'd say our success rate is about eighty percent."

While today sex is more open and accepted, it is often more pressured and stressed. Over and over, psychiatrists and psychologists told us that women really want romance. They want sex that is part of love and romance. This means holding, small loving gestures and a real desire to please one another. When sex is satisfying, the other angers of life can be easier to handle and less bothersome.

6

The Real Truth About Happily Ever After

In marriage, we may hold our anger in because we are afraid to let it out. So we put on an act. We pretend not to be angry. We pretend sexual desire when it has been blown out by anger.

"Just forget it. I don't want to talk about it," a woman may shout. While we may wish to forget, our anger inevitably influences our relationship.

The irony is that anger becomes more destructive to our marriage the more we try to hide it. When feelings are acknowledged and spoken about freely anger flows, but also forgiving and forgetting naturally take place. When anger is not expressed, it festers and builds; resentment, emotional distance and coldness slowly take over.

"I was single for fifteen years and have just been married a year and a half," a wardrobe specialist explained. "When I was single, anger was easier to handle. I just went home or if I had an argument with a boyfriend, I'd get in the car and go for a drive, but now we're married and living in a city apartment. You're closed in here like a couple of rams."

The intimacy of marriage forces us to deal with our angry feelings. Many women think intimacy "just grows." But intimacy does not automatically come. Marriage provides only familiarity, not intimacy. Intimacy is possible only when we are absolutely ourselves, not putting on an act to please another person. Only when we are intimate—when we do feel completely accepted and loved—is anger in marriage successfully managed. Intimacy, honesty and a resolution of anger are constant goals.

Anger is present in all marriages, everyone knows this. But what is really normal? How can we distinguish a neurotic need from a legitimate anger? What feelings are to be expected? When, on the other hand, are destructive forces eating away at our marriage?

The answers to these questions are often clouded because women frequently confuse anger with the absence of love. Therefore, they feel enormous guilt at being truly angry at a loved one and try to hide their anger.

A thirty-year-old woman explained, "Early in my marriage, when I got angry, my husband's first question was always, 'Do you still love me?' I'd say, 'What the hell does that mean?' Then I realized he felt threatened. I had to keep reassuring him. In my family, when my parents became angry with me, I always knew it was directed at what I had done. It was the act they were angry at. I never felt unloved so I'm not ashamed of showing anger as an adult. I know I'm not removing love."

This woman is unusual. Too often we suppress our angry feelings, telling ourselves:

"It's not worth an argument."

"He won't change anyway."

"It's hopeless, we disagree on so many things."

One very confident actress admitted, "Most of the time, I sit on my anger for at least twenty-four hours. And believe me, that's an improvement. I used to sit on it for years!"

Unfortunately, what happens when we suppress our anger and later express it, is that our anger just does not disappear. It seems to go on and on. "I just can't forgive him; I can't get it out of my mind," may be the feeling. The trouble with hiding anger is that it just doesn't work. As a minister's wife explained, "Not talking, moping around or being bitchy just doesn't work. I know, I've tried it." Once repressed, anger can never be totally resolved. So the idea is to express anger promptly. Of course, this is easy to say but very difficult to do.

Most frequently, the cause of our anger is not a major problem but small things that tend to accumulate.

In marriage, small angers have a way of sneaking up and causing big anger. Psychologists tell us that most marriage anger is not the result of great tragedies but rather an accumulation of minor irritations. The women we spoke with strongly confirmed this. Almost everyone mentioned a stream of small things, but things that recurred over and over. Usually, these centered on a recurring theme: one person finding the other stingy, secretive, unromantic, dull or selfish.

Hidden attitudes were mentioned over and over. A forty-two-year-old teacher said, "I feel my husband thinks he's better and more important than I am because of his position as a medical person compared to my only being a teacher. It's subtle but it makes me furious."

Another woman commented, "My husband won't eat out or make himself a meal so I'm always watching the clock. I have to be home for him. His mother was always home and he expects it. He leaves every dish in the sink. He really believes he should be served and I should clean up. These are small annoyances but we don't seem to be able to work them out."

The bathroom may seem a small, even silly issue. But it can cause great tensions. The bathroom is one of the first places we learn to gain control of our physical selves. When a bathroom is "messed up," it's as though we have lost control. When our mate leaves the cap off the toothpaste, fuzzes the sink with beard clippings, or coats the bowl with shaving cream, we may feel attacked and disrupted. The hair in the sink can begin to symbolize the entire person. Conveniently, it may become a place to hang all our hidden grievances and anger.

Not being listened to may seem like a small thing, but it can create tremendous anger.

While traditionally women have been the nurturers and listeners, today we realize that women need their husbands to listen too. When emotional support is absent, anger results. The woman is not only stuck with her original frustration but also has self-doubts that perhaps her demands are just childish or over-emotional.

How much "understanding" from a mate can we expect? Psychologists say having someone to rely on and confide in is a basic prerequisite for mental health, not some infantile fantasy. but experts warn us not to overexpect. We should feel good being able to express our thoughts honestly, but getting the response we want simply may not happen.

"One of pop psychology's very destructive myths," explains Dr. Howard I. Glazer, Ph.D., Professor of Psychology at Cornell University Medical College, "is the overemphasis on how to make demands, with the implication that if you just learn how to do it right, you'll get what you want. But the simple truth is that however you beg, plead or demand, people won't do what you want them to do unless it fits in with what they want to do themselves."

Many of us, perhaps most, have trouble expressing anger because we have no good examples to follow. One woman, whose mother was a dentist and father a lawyer, explained, "My parents were so busy, I rarely saw them and I never saw them fight. The first time I had a fight with my husband, I thought we'd have to get a divorce. My mother was raised never to express anger and she never did. I remember when I was a teenager, she got so mad at me, she didn't speak to me for a week. But to this day, she's never talked about it."

Unfortunately, there are no guidelines for knowing just how many small complaints, how much bickering, are "okay" in a marriage. Sometimes talking about small things can be a defense mechanism, a way to deal with feelings of insecurity. Or it may be a pushing away mechanism, a defense against too much closeness. Fighting over small things can also be the means by which two people fight for power in a marriage. If one partner dominates the other, frequently the one on the losing end will become angry and start to bicker. For example, if a wife feels completely overpowered by her husband and afraid to confront major differences, she may start to fight over small things.

In a marriage, nothing is more crucial than trust. We want to feel, "He will be there when I need him." Only with trust comes honest communication and a real resolution of anger. Trust is often destroyed by small, everyday disappointments. A thirty-five-year-old teacher, married for six years, reflected the feelings of many women we interviewed:

> "When we got married, I felt Greg was my best friend. I just don't feel that anymore. There have been too many disappointments, too many times he wasn't there when I needed him, too many times he didn't come through.
>
> "When we got engaged, Greg asked me what I wanted, I said a ring, of course, I had always wanted a diamond. But he gave me an opal. 'How was I supposed to know you wanted a diamond?' he asked. I was bitterly disappointed. It took me five years to get up my courage to tell him about that lousy opal.
>
> "When my first child was born, I was devastated when he didn't give me a gift. He should have bought me something. I didn't tell him for years but I also didn't forgive him for years.

"It wasn't the thing. It was the thought. I had a need and he had no idea. We were on totally different wavelengths.

"I'm always disappointed in the way he does things. This summer, I had to nag him over and over to put up some molding. You know what finally happened. I was left with big holes in the wall and the molding still wasn't straight. I feel if I want something done right I always have to do it myself. He *always* disappoints me.

" 'You like to tear me down, nothing I do is right,' he always says. But he sets himself up for it. If I send him to the toy store, it never fails. He will buy something our child can't use or a duplication of something we have. It happens over and over.

"If I ask him to do something, I never trust him to do it. I'm never sure that he will and that makes me uncomfortable and nervous. Then I'm angry that he's made me feel so anxious.

"I know it's all small things. But it adds up. It accumulates. The result is not only anger. It is a loss of love."

One recently engaged thirty-year-old shipping executive said of her fiance, "I trust him one hundred percent and I've never trusted anyone. Outside of my parents, he's the only one I've ever trusted completely with my feelings or with myself." In previous relationships, her lack of trust, she said, always added a "tremendous strain" and eventual anger.

Jane, a successful singer whose husband is a businessman, explained her feelings this way:

"I absolutely never count on my husband. I think there are very, very few people you can count on in this world. I have one good friend. I always feel if there were some crisis, some emergency, I could turn to her. But my husband...never. Why? Because throughout our ten years of marriage whenever I have needed him, he's always let me down.

"Of course, there's always a good reason. He was working. He was out of town. There was *always* something. Emotionally, when I've needed him, he's never been helpful. So now I don't depend. It's a reflex already. The trouble is I don't feel close either. It killed something. Sometimes I wonder if it killed my love."

As Maj-Britt Rosenbaum, M.D., Associate Professor of Clinical Psychiatry at Montefiore Hospital and Medical Center in New York City, put it, "Most simply, in marriage, you must dare to be yourself and show your feelings as much as possible, despite the risks involved. Of course, that means continuing to communicate with your partner. Relationships often get into trouble because feelings that are deemed unacceptable are closed off: 'I can't tell him *that*...it might hurt our relationship', we may think."

Trust also affects the sexual relationship. Many people believe that orgasm co-relates very closely with the trust a woman feels in her sexual partner. If you are angry, wary or suspicious, you will constantly be trying to keep control. This has a very negative effect on sexual satisfaction.

"We'd be just fine if only he would..." "If he would just change the way he..." "If I could just rely on him to..." Over and over, these thoughts were expressed by women we interviewed. They blamed their husbands for their problems. Indeed this might be the case. Some husbands *are* more difficult to live with than others. Unfortunately, however, the only way to decrease marriage problems is to seek solutions for habits that will not, probably cannot, change.

"I got married for all the wrong reasons," we often heard women say. In truth, all of us get married for a bunch of right reasons and a bunch of wrong reasons. Indeed, these wrong reasons might be right for us. They may fill an important need.

Despite women's liberation, a woman, for the most part, still needs to get married more than a man. A girl who feels she does not have the physical or intellectual characteristics to get a man she really wants may settle for someone who "asks her." Later, she may feel trapped and angry.

All people get married in part to avoid being alone. As one woman told us:

> "I had a thirty-one-year-old friend who got breast cancer and had to have her breast removed. She was single. Her parents had died. I saw her and I was afraid for myself. I never wanted to be alone like that. Shortly thereafter, I convinced Lonny to get married."

Because a woman may be dependent on her husband, however, she may not feel free to express her anger. Instead she may say and do only what she feels will be accepted. Such self-effacement inevitably produces just more anger, tensions and misunderstandings. "I have a hard time getting anger out," a thirty-eight-year-old divorced mother of one admitted. "I was brought up that you don't get angry. When I get angry, I always feel I have to apologize. 'I don't want to argue,' was a classic line in my marriage. And look what happened."

While suppression is often a calculated response, the results may not be what we expect, as Mary, a forty-eight-year-old woman, explained:

> "I spent my first marriage keeping my mouth shut. According to my first husband, I didn't do anything right. I didn't walk right. I didn't talk right. I didn't cook right. But I never spoke up. I was desperately trying to hold on. Of course, it never worked. I grew to hate my first husband.
>
> "I made up my mind that if my second husband did something wrong, I would say it right then and there. I don't wait. I don't care if we are in public. If we are at a restaurant with friends, I'll say, 'Don't look at me like that.' If he's making me uncomfortable I don't even care if it embarrasses others. It works for us. It erases the anger. We've been married fifteen years."

For the most part, however, we suppress our anger unconsciously. Real feelings and real anger are put down so quickly and quietly, many women are not even aware of the anger. Rather than face the anger, a woman will become depressed, physically ill or just helpless.

If you are angry at your husband but don't express this anger, ask yourself why not. Are you hiding this anger—pretending things don't bother you? When you're afraid of opening up in front of a mate, but are able to do so with others, it may mean you don't really trust him. You're afraid that he might hurt you further or retaliate.

As difficult as it sounds, you should point out how his presence inhibits you. Not being your natural self takes up enormous energy. Expressing yourself honestly takes courage. It is not easy. But it gets easier the more you become accustomed to responding to your feelings. And it will be worth it.

The Controlling Husband. If you are trying to deal with a controlling husband, you probably feel deeply angry but don't understand why. A controlling person attempts to ward off hurts and anger by elaborate mental manipulations.

If you are angry at a controlling husband, he probably has an annoying habit of turning things around. Somehow he proves an anger-inducing incident was really *your* fault. The hurt inflicted on you wasn't really a hurt at all, but your own shortcomings finally brought to life by his generous behavior. You may feel confused and not sure exactly how to retaliate.

Controlling people can be extremely difficult to deal with because they are so far removed from their own feelings. They are not really honest. Worse yet, they will not accept their dishonesty and so give defensive excuses when cornered. They lure you away from any meaningful discussion of their feelings, their anger or their weak points.

When controlling people do show anger, it is extraordinarily unpleasant. One has the feeling of being in the same room with a tyrant. A controlling man cannot say, "You hurt me." Instead they lash out in torrents of rage.

Frequently, money becomes the weapon. A man may overpower with his power of the purse, a woman may then overspend, compulsively shopping to "get back at him." "My husband controls through money," explained a forty-year-old woman. "I am totally financially dependent. I do not work. I do not want to. Each morning he will say, 'How much money do you need today?' I feel that is not only control, it is abuse. It is never *our* money. It is *his* money. When the bills come in, he has a fit and he threatens to take away my charge cards. I never really know how much money we have. He keeps it mysterious. That makes me angry. I never know if he's holding back because of finances or emotions."

"He'll never buy something just for me. When I complain I would like a fur coat, he says, 'How can you complain? Do you have such a bad life?' Of course, I have a good life. It's not really the fur coat either. I don't even care about the coat. But whenever he spends money, it is always something he can enjoy. A fur coat would be just for me. I tell him, 'You don't buy it because you can't wear it.' It seems he'll never want to do it just for me and I'll always feel badly about it."

Some women with tremendous amounts of anger may "blame" their husbands. In fact, they are also furious at themselves for falling short of their own mark.

The Perfectionist Wife. "I'm not a perfectionist," one woman protested. "In fact, I'm rather careless and sloppy."

But perfectionism is not, as many assume, a wish to have a perfect product. The perfectionist is a compulsive striver. She nags herself with her failures and completely ignores her successes. She allows herself no relief from self-condemnation. The perfectionist cannot win. She is always convinced of her own stupidity and inadequacy.

One of the worst aspects of perfectionism is we may become

paralyzed—afraid to move in any direction. High standards are wonderful as long as they work for us. What is bad is when these goals block ourselves or drive others away.

The dark side of perfectionism is a source of much marriage anger and self-anguish. When we try to accomplish the impossible, our only reward becomes the sour taste of frustration and failure. We become angry at ourselves and we splash this anger all over others.

When our goals are too high, we never allow ourselves to succeed. As Dr. David D. Burns writes in *Feeling Good: The New Mood Therapy*, "The harder you strive for perfection, the worse your disappointment will become, because it's only an abstraction, a concept that doesn't fit reality. Everything can be improved if you look at it closely and critically enough— every person, idea, work of art, experience, *everything*. So if you are a perfectionist, you are a guaranteed loser in whatever you do. In pursuit of riches, you earn only misery."

Why then do so many women go around banging their heads against this impossible wall, injuring their husbands and families as well as themselves? Psychiatrists say we often pursue unrealistic dreams because of a misplaced belief that our worth is measured in terms of these accomplishments. If I get an A on an exam, if I have a higher salary, if I have a bigger, prettier house, then I feel I'm worth more as a person. This type of person feels she must achieve in order to be loved. Since we inevitably fall short of impossible standards, we become furious with ourselves.

Most experts believe that perfectionism begins in childhood, probably from a blocking of early needs for love and acceptance. Psychiatrists tell us that such damage occurs when a parent reacts to a child's inevitable mistakes and failures in a personal way or nervously worries, "What's *wrong* with her?"

The child gets the message. Don't fail. Don't make mistakes. Since this is impossible, the child becomes anxious—anxious about the test, anxious about camp, anxious about almost everything. And the anxious child inevitably becomes the insecure and angry adult.

While perfectionism affects our entire lives, the real damage is to our marriage and family. Such women are so busy thinking about all the things they did wrong, they cannot enjoy the present. The disillusionment that a husband is not their fantasy prince makes them go to the other extreme and he becomes an ogre. While berating others but mostly themselves, these women keep people, even a husband, at a distance. They tend to put a wall around themselves, afraid they will be found wanting in some way. True feelings are hidden for so long and sometimes so successfully, after a while they feel nothing at all. A deadness is created.

If we feel angry but are too fearful to communicate directly with the person causing the anger, it is beneficial to talk to someone, to be able to tell someone what is really bothering you. "If I don't talk to someone, I'll explode," may be the feeling. A discharge of negative feelings can be very helpful, but it can also intensify, rather than diminish, anger. *IT DEPENDS TO WHOM YOU TALK.*

For some couples, inappropriate third party communication can bring disaster.

Meya and Tom were such a couple. Because Meya never felt she could confront Tom directly, she developed a pattern of complaining to everyone she knew about him. She told everyone and anyone who would listen just how bad she thought her life was.

Friends loved to hear this "inside dope." But after going over and over her resentments, Meya never really got the kind of support that made her feel better, nor did she come to a better understanding of the sources of her unhappiness. In fact, all that happened was her friends started to regard her in a "funny" way which she immediately felt. They began to avoid her. She felt shunned, excluded. Further, the friends who did give advice seemed to take sides. This only added fuel to her anger.

Worst of all, even when Meya and Tom were able to patch up their difficulties, Tom would find that everyone around knew their problems. He resented it bitterly. So another battle would begin.

Many women with marital problems are better off talking to a professional. In therapy, nasty feelings can be discussed without risk of further harm. Couple therapy deals with problems in a marriage relationship.

To find out how couple therapy works, we spoke with Barbara Feld, M.S.W., a licensed family therapist who sees couples and families in private practice in New York City. She also directed the family therapy center at Montefiore Hospital and Medical Center in the Bronx for many years.

"People come to couple therapy in many different ways. Usually one person is very unhappy and calls for therapy alone. Depending on the problem, the therapist may feel that while personal difficulties exist, there is also a lot going on in the marriage that may be contributing to the difficulties.

"For example, recently a colleague called and said she had a friend, a young woman in her early thirties who was always falling and hurting herself. She had no children and was married to an extremely successful man who would often go off to Europe, leaving her alone. While she was financially very comfortable, she was exceedingly unhappy.

"When I heard this story, I felt that if she's always hurting herself and if her husband is always working, there must be something going on in their marriage which she may be afraid to confront and which is causing her unhappiness. So I asked her to come in and talk. Having spoken with her, I then suggested that she come in with her husband. She said, 'I'd like to but he absolutely won't.' This is not unusual.

"So we talked about some ways to get him to come in. Some women ask their husbands in such a negative fashion, the men naturally don't want to come. Sometimes a woman subconsciously fears her husband and keeps him from coming. We talked about more positive approaches, such as saying, 'I think therapy would help us be happier together.' It is very important to avoid blaming or pointing a finger. Some couples realize they are fighting a great deal and decide mutually to come for therapy. They may have tried but been unable to change things. From my experience, though, I find women are more likely to seek help. Usually, a woman will overtly recognize her unhappiness, while a man may just bury himself in his work or have an affair.

"How does couple therapy work? I'll give you an example. Of course, this couple will be a composite since all therapy is strictly confidential.

"This couple, in their early forties, were having marital difficulties, although it was immediately apparent to me that their bond was strong. They cared very much for each other and had been together fifteen years. The woman, who is herself a lawyer, felt that her husband was too involved in his business. Even when he came home, only business was on his mind. She wanted him to share his day with her, his feelings, his thoughts about what went on. But he never shared these things. They had very different styles. Of course, different styles are fine. But the trouble was she felt extremely neglected. She interpreted his lack of communication as indifference and was deeply hurt by it.

"In working with a couple, the first thing I try to get clear is the problem. Exactly what is the problem, how long has it been going on, what has the couple tried to do about it? Have they ever talked to each other about it? (This varies considerably since it is safer and often easier to say nothing.) Very often, I will hear that couples have talked, even fought about the problem. However, they usually concentrate on specifics. Even when these specifics are worked out, they are left feeling unhappy.

"What I try to do in the first few sessions is to see the parallels for their feelings in their families or origin. Sometimes the extent of the rage a person feels does not really belong to the person they married but comes from old unmet needs from the past. This is a basic principle of couple therapy. The partners will find in each other something that hurt them from their past and then react to each other as though they were still the child reacting to the parent. Their feelings may have the intensity of their feelings as a young child.

"This woman, now a successful lawyer, may be feeling neglected by her husband because she felt neglected by her father or mother. 'Does this present feeling remind you of any similar feeling from your past?' I may ask. The woman may then remember her childhood. In this case, this woman's mother had been working in the family store and also raising six other children. She had little time for this girl. By recalling her upbringing, this woman begins to see how her feelings of neglect are being repeated in her marriage. She begins to realize that the intensity does not really belong to her husband.

"This is not the end of the story, however. We then look into the parallels for him. I try to understand with the man what his family relationship was. With this man, he told me that as a boy, he'd come home from school and go to his room and do his homework. He had no real intimate contact with either of his parents. His own parents had a strained marriage filled with uncomfortable silences, and his way of dealing with this was just to retreat and avoid everyone.

"As each spouse tells his or her story, I listen and watch. I watch the individual's expression and the spouse's reaction. Sometimes, I will direct the story by asking for a clarification. If the spouse seems sympathetic, I might stop and point this out to the couple. They now become aware that they may be repeating their patterns of childhood. For instance, this husband's fear of closeness may again be causing him to retreat.

"How does all of this help? First, it makes the wife realize that her husband's way of reacting may not mean he does not care about her, or that she is an unworthy person. It becomes very clear that this is his pattern. It is the only way he knows to react. In their marriage, however, her needs may not mesh with this approach.

"What happens when people are dating is an unspoken but yet understood promise that each person will meet the other's needs, making up for all the hurts of the past. Unfortunately, this is an impossible expectation. Because it is expected, however, the disappointment can be very great. Somehow it seems very needy people end up with other very needy people. Each gets angry their needs are not met.

"Let me go back to this woman's mother for a minute. Although her mother had met all her physical needs, she had no energy left for this girl's emotional needs. Because she feels needy, she was hoping to find someone who would meet these needs AT LAST.

"By going back to our childhood, we get a better idea of the roots of the intensity of our feelings: his need to keep away and her intense pull for closeness.

"Once they have talked about their backgrounds and have seen how they intertwined, they can begin to understand. The hurt and rage starts to calm down as they take things less personally.

"Understanding does not happen right away, however. It takes a while. For this couple, understanding took about four sessions. Then they had to build from there. Just because they understood, they could not change their behavior overnight or trust each other so quickly.

"So during therapy, we begin to work on specifics. We try to reach some compromises they both can live with.

"With a couple like this, we finished therapy in about six months. I feel they left therapy with a greater understanding of the source of their hurts, a more basic recognition that pain from our childhood cannot be made up by another adult, but a realization that compromises can be found to satisfy many of our needs. A couple like this may feel closer, more relaxed and less angry, their marriage will be on a firmer, more satisfying foundation."

The specifics about couple therapy include:

COST: Private therapy can cost from $40 to $150 per session. This may be covered by insurance. If an insurance policy provides for psychiatric counseling, couple therapy is probably also covered. About half of all couples pay for their treatment through their insurance.

Due to today's economic pressures, many people try to avoid therapy until their difficulties are very bad. It is better, and sometimes less expensive, to get help early.

TIME INVOLVED: A therapist usually meets with a couple once a week for fifty minutes. Couple therapy can take from three months to two to three years.

WHEN TO GO: It is easier to deal with marital problems in the early stages of marriage, the first few years, and before a couple has built up a great deal of pain.

How do you know when you need couple therapy? Couples who are unable to talk things out and make changes that are comfortable for both of them may find such therapy very helpful. If the relationship is bringing unhappiness to one or both of them, couple therapy can only improve the situation.

GROUP OR INDIVIDUAL: The therapy mode varies depending on the personalities and problems involved. Sometimes people are seen first on an individual basis, private sessions are then intermingled with joint sessions. Often they meet individually because one or both people find it difficult or impossible to unburden themselves in front of each other. Sometimes only joint sessions are held.

Couples groups may also be recommended. A group usually consists of four other couples, of differing ages and backgrounds, led by a therapist. Different types of couples are put together since this gives an opportunity to see very different perspectives on common problems. Couples are usually not put into a group if they still have a great deal of overt rage. Most are seen individually at the beginning. And some couples are never placed in groups.

It is very important to remember that anger in marriage is neither new nor bad. In 42 B.C. Publius wrote, "The anger of lovers renews the strength of love." Psychiatrists say a second marriage partner is usually selected for similar neurotic reasons as the first. It is not that the second partner is so different from the first. But the anger from old hurts does not exist. When anger flows freely, we can renegotiate our marriage without changing partners.

Anger is also a tool for growth. Especially today, a married woman is not content to just rely on the "Mrs." myth of fulfillment. Certainly, the question is rather how she can lead her life with positive feelings about herself and fulfillment. Anger—when it is directed and on target—is an important tool in this struggle to change and grow.

Over and over in conversations with married women, we found what they sought most was a sympathetic, supportive listener. Because few women express their feelings openly, perceptive listening is needed.

If we hear a chorus of vague and varied complaints, we might suspect that unresolved angers are the real problem. Most of the time, this anger results not from the cacophony of a disordered mind, but when a stable person becomes unable to ventilate repressed emotions. By listening, not just to our husbands but to ourselves as well, we can begin to discover and consciously express our real feelings more honestly and openly.

7

Living With Children: Learning About Anger

M ost little girls dream about becoming mommies. They practice with dolls, pretty dolls that make the little girls feel pretty and good about themselves.

When little girls grow up and have their own children, problems they never expected nor wanted may present themselves. Hurt and disappointment result. Anger seeps in.

Jane is eleven. She is the oldest of three children. Her mother, age thirty-four and a full-time housewife, was divorced and is remarried. Jane is her first-born from her previous marriage.

"Jane is eleven. My dad says there is always a needy child. Well, Jane is my needy child. I feel like she's never happy and I want her to be happy. It's that indefinable happy. I want her to be accepted by her friends, be popular, be smart. Well, Jane just seems to have trouble in all these areas. Now she tells me she's eating lunch alone in the cafeteria. I asked her if it was her choice or her friends'. She says a little of both, but I know the truth. Jane just is not popular with the other girls and I don't know how to help. I've tried everything. If she wants a certain pocketbook, a certain pair of jeans, I buy it. I would not spend that money on myself. I'd think twice. But I desperately want her to feel better. She seems to wear her insecurity on her sleeve. She sort of sidles up to the kids and asks, 'Will you be my friend?' Well, do you know what they say? They say no. And it hurts. It positively crushes her.

"I sent her to camp and things seemed much better at the beginning. It was a whole new group of girls. I thought it was going to be a whole new start. But before long, it was the same story all over again.

"Sometimes I feel she's just a malcontent: I work twice as hard trying to make her happy as anyone else. You know how many things we've tried. First art, then dance, photography, needlework, cooking, tennis. It's all been awful.

"I worry about her. To be honest, I'm also very angry at her. She is a drain on my life. It's so all-consuming when your child has a problem.

"I get angry because it is an enormous responsibility that I really never wanted. If she didn't have these problems, I wouldn't have to walk around so tense and nervous. I'm always worried. I'm always half-holding my breath, waiting for the next crisis. I hate that feeling. Sometimes I'm furious at her for making my life strained."

Jennifer is thirty-five. Married to a surgeon, she was a librarian but is not working now. They do not have children.

"I always thought that if I wanted children, I'd have children. We've been trying for over three years and it's just not working. I've had one miscarriage and the doctors are now saying there may be a problem. Of course, I always knew about difficulties but I never thought it would happen to me. I feel a lot of anger at how difficult the whole process is becoming. The longer I go without, the more I say it's not the end of the world. But I never know what's happening. I find *that* is the frustrating thing—the uncertainty."

Barbara is extremely pretty with clear blue eyes and a refreshing natural look. She is her club's top tennis player in both the men's and women's divisions. Barbara is thirty-eight and has two children.

"Losing a child has made me very angry. The anger stems from helplessness and a feeling of why her? Why me? There is a lot of anger in not being given a choice.

"When my first child was six months old, we were told she had leukemia and would die. She lived eighteen months. It was six years ago, but I still think about her every day. And I still cry every day.

"People would say, 'How are you?' and I'd say, 'Lousy, how do you think I am?' The experience freed my tongue. Before, I kept it all inside. Now I say what I feel.

"I think the only thing that saved my marriage was that we each blamed ourselves rather than the other. I felt I must have done something wrong. As a mother, you are supposed to protect your child and I couldn't protect my child. My husband blamed himself, never me. I am not sure why.

"I still feel angry because I can't find the right place for this in my life. I have very strong feelings about never being the same. It is the most important thing that has happened to me. It affects me every day of my life. Yet when people say, 'How many children do you have?' I do not feel I can say three and then, when they ask, I say one is dead. So I say two but I don't feel totally comfortable. I just can't erase her like that.

"I'm still angry about things that happened during that time. It seemed most people said or did the wrong thing. Doctors were absolutely cruel. They kept me waiting for hours and then would stroll in without an apology. I was holding a dying baby in my arms who needed treatment. She needed continual blood tests. It was a matter of life or death. But the doctors didn't call me back for hours. They'd keep me waiting. I still think it was wrong. They made me leave the room. They said I made them nervous.

"One day when my daughter was particularly sick, I asked a friend to take me home from the hospital. I could not face a taxi. She kept me waiting for two hours while she ran errands. It was not right. She should have taken me home if she was my friend. I felt people should have bent over backwards. But they didn't.

"What helped? Nothing helped. After she died, I couldn't believe I was still alive. It was hard to get out of bed in the morning.

"Well, some people did help. But it was not easy to find help. The hospital put me in a mother's group but the children were not dying. It made me even angrier. Why did they put me in that group? I didn't belong. They certainly knew the situation. Eventually, I did get a very good therapist and he helped. I had a rabbi who understood. He came to the hospital at three a.m. Most importantly of all, he didn't give advice. He acknowledged my feelings. My anger is still there, though. It is not as bad now. But I don't think it will ever go away completely."

Handling the difficulties children present can be difficult—at times, we may feel, impossible. But coping is essential because a disturbed parent-child relationship will not only make *us* angry, it will deeply affect our children.

If we try to hide our anger and become depressed we may do our children more harm than if we act "insanely" angry. A fascinating study of children of psychotic mothers found they were less affected than children of depressed mothers. While a depressed mother may recover one hundred percent, her children may show the effects for years.

Anger at our children comes, in part, from having our own

lives disrupted. In late 1981, the *Ladies Home Journal* polled 30,000 readers on marriage and family life. As far as children were concerned, both men and women felt children often put a damper on marriage, frequently souring rather than complementing it. The poll showed that married women with children are less optimistic about the future, feel they have less control over their lives, become irritable far more easily, tend to have less sex, and tend to enjoy what sex they have less than they did before their children were born.

Certainly, the old notion that a child cements a marriage, bringing a wandering husband home, is folly. A child can cause tension in a previously harmonious and happy marriage.

A twenty-six-year-old massage therapist and mother of an infant explained, "I'm always giving up. I have to give up for my baby. I give up for my husband. I give up for my work. I often wonder, when am I going to get it all back? But I feel, as a woman, it is expected of me. Women still have to take care of the baby. They still have the job of the home and they still have the job of maintaining the relationship. I always have to say to my husband, 'Tell me how you fell.' For me, it's non-ending. I feel drained at having to keep everyone happy all the time."

Much anger is due to financial pressures. Raising a child today is expensive (as if parents need to be told this). But even the most practical parent may be amazed at just how expensive. According to the U.S. Department of Agriculture, allowing for an eight percent annual inflation rate, it now costs more than $134,000 to support a child to age eighteen—nearly four times the cost, $34,174, for a child born in 1960. And this does not include education beyond high school! With private colleges costing over $10,000 each year, the figures are staggering. It inevitably means sacrifice for the parents.

Money and children, in that order, are the most frequently cited reasons for the breakup of second marriages (forty-four percent of remarriages end in divorce). But these are not necessarily two separate issues since child care costs (especially where there are offspring from more than one marriage) are a major part of most family budgets.

Anger also comes from disappointment. Sometimes our children's personalities or abilities are not those we fantasized. Susan, a forty-two-year-old church organist and mother of two boys aged seven and eleven, confessed, "When they were babies, I was annoyed but I can't really remember getting angry. I get angrier as their personalities develop and traits become more a part of them as individuals. There is a disappointment if they are not turning out like you'd like. You get more annoyed at some little thing."

When a woman draws her sense of identity from her children, anger is inevitable.

Caroline was a perfect example. She was an unmarried woman who, although attractive, had difficulties at work and in relationships with men. As a young woman, Caroline dated older men. They were easier to relate to and sexually more exciting. Still unmarried at thirty, Caroline decided to have a child, desperately wanting "to have something." When Caroline found her baby did not fulfill many adult needs, she became deeply disappointed. She was now facing her own problems as well as those of her baby.

Interestingly, Caroline would often become ill, and frequently had to be hospitalized. Doctors felt these were psychosomatic complaints, most likely an almost classic case of misdirected anger.

Anger is also due to frustration—not knowing exactly how to act and react to our children. "I feel so impotent," one mother confided to me. "You can talk yourself blue in the face. It doesn't help. Jill is thirteen. She wants to wear make-up one minute and the next minute she wants to curl up with her Snoopy. When she goes to school and another kid destroys her, I can't make it right."

One of the most difficult things about raising children is knowing when to hold the reins and when to let go. It is especially difficult because we have to keep shifting gears. For example, in babies, the best way to build independence paradoxically is to let them be as dependent as they like. "Studies show that the more dependent and close you permit children to be in the first year or two of life," says New York psychologist Louise J. Kaplan, "the less anxious they are likely to be as they move into the world at two, three and four." One New York City psychiatrist explained a parent must distinguish between limiting children and punishing them. He explained, "Children must be contained. A parent must be limiting but not in a punitive way."

As parents, we must strive to have our children respect and heed our restrictions without resenting us too much. It means walking a delicate line.

When children meet our hopes and dreams, there is little anger. " 'You won't have a minute's trouble with this one,' the nurse told me," a fifty-four-year-old woman recalled. "She was absolutely right. My daughter was a pleasure from the moment she was born. She was pretty. She was very bright. She was always well-liked. Even in adolescence, we didn't have those usual battles."

However, when problems with children are severe—a genetically defective child, for example—the parent's anger can be intense. This anger is suffered by thousands. Almost ten percent of American children are afflicted with a serious genetic disease; one out of every three pediatric hospital admissions is for a genetic problem.

Edwin Goldstein, M.D., a psychiatrist who counsels couples at Columbia Presbyterian Hospital in New York City, explains what can happen:

"One of the typical immediate responses is withdrawal—

between husband and wife, the couple and other family members, the couple and their friends. Many times, they find they are soon not talking to each other. They feel blamed or they do, in fact, blame each other."

It is worth noting that the woman usually gets the worse end of things. In some cultures, it is always regarded as the woman's fault when such a child is born. In these cultures, it is also considered a disgrace. For couples coming from such backgrounds, the marital strain can be devastating. The man may openly blame his wife (although biologically this is not accurate). Unwilling to deal with the situation, he often walks out leaving her alone with the baby.

The sexual relationship in the surviving marriages may be seriously strained. There is often a loss of desire, avoidance and impotence. This heightens the woman's feelings of rejection and loss of acceptance. Fights occur in which genetic medical information provided at the hospital is used cruelly.

Such intense and inevitable anger is both complex and chronic. Dr. F. Clarke Fraser, M.D., Director of Medical Genetics at Montreal Children's Hospital, gave one helpful suggestion, "I have found a useful line to be, 'You know, we all carry several deleterious genes, and most of us are simply lucky enough not to know about them. You are not inferior just because you happen to know about yours. Your spouse is carrying just as many.' "

With the current divorce epidemic, we may "inherit" the problems of other women's children.

The frustrations of Carol Anthony, a scientist, mother of a three-year-old daughter and step-mother of three teenage sons, are very common:

"The boys are with us on the weekends and most of the time they are here, I'm angry. I think the reason is I feel caught and I feel powerless. I'm not the boys' real mother so I can't just yell if they do something that annoys me. I'm always aware they are not mine. That stops me. It shuts me up. But it also makes me angry. What happens is there is usually a scene over something small, usually unrelated to the real problem. Of course, we never discuss the real problem. It's too risky and hurtful for everyone. And would it help? I really don't want to hear that they honestly like their mother better.

"With my own child, everything is different. There is nothing stopping me. I can get mad at the baby or complain about getting up in the middle of the night. The complaining somehow washes away the anger. It's only when I feel stifled that I explode."

Children have pent-up anger too. Often they cannot let it out at adults. As Dr. Leo Madow, Chairman of the Department of Psychiatry at the Medical College of Pennsylvania and author of the book *Anger*, explains, "At the core of unexpressed anger is the fear of losing love. This threat of withdrawing love is terrifying especially to a child. So if Mommy and Daddy tell you to be nice and not make a fuss, the child will try to please them regardless of how she feels."

Girls generally are less able to deal directly with their anger than boys. According to Dr. Helen De Rosis, an associate clinical professor of psychiatry at New York University School of Medicine, a subtle difference in upbringing causes this phenomena. "While little boys are encouraged to stand up for themselves and fight, little girls usually aren't permitted to punch, scream, or yell—it's not ladylike. To be angry is active and it's okay for boys; girls, however, are expected to be timid and passive. While society's attitudes are slowly changing, we are still affected by these stereotypes."

When children are angry, they attack those with less power: children with personalities weaker than their own. All of us have seen the cruelties children foist on one another. Some people believe children are cruel because they don't know any better. But if you observe children closely, there is no doubt they know exactly what they are doing.

When children feel their anger is unacceptable, they will use a defense mechanism to reduce the anxiety produced. Rather than getting angry, children may have sick and dying fantasies. Their thinking is, "I'll get sick and die and they will all be standing around my bed and boy, will they be sorry."

All of us from the age of five or six use some defense mechanisms, what Freud called "classical ego defenses." These include:

WITHDRAWAL: A very common defense mechanism in young children. It is the most direct defense possible. If a situation seems too difficult, the child simply gets out of it or runs away from it (either physically or mentally).

DISPLACEMENT: This entails substituting a person or object for the real source of anger. For example, a boy may be angry with his father but cannot admit this fully to himself because he loves and depends on his father. Therefore he displaces this anger, aggression and anxiety onto an imaginary tiger or goblin which he thinks will eat him up.

DENIAL: Denial is the refusal to admit that a feeling exists or that an event happened. For example, children may react to the death of a favorite pet by pretending the pet is still living in the house and sleeping with them at night.

REPRESSION: Repression is an extreme form of denial in which children completely erase a frightening event or feeling from their awareness. They do not need to rely on fantasy since they literally do not remember that the feeling ever occurred.

REACTION FORMATION: Reaction formation occurs when children have thoughts or desires that make them anxious and react against these thoughts by behaving in the opposite extreme. For example, a child who is angry about having a new baby in the house may excessively kiss and hug the baby.

RATIONALIZATION: A very common adult defense mechanism, rationalization is used less frequently by children since it requires verbal skill and a knowledge of social rules. With rationalization, people make unacceptable behavior or thoughts "respectable" by inventing a socially acceptable explanation for them. For example, a child may say, "I had to hit my baby sister because she was being bad and needed to be taught a lesson."

At a very young age, children learn to inhibit their anger. They develop a coping style. Most preschool children use several defense mechanisms. Very rarely does a child choose one and use it exclusively. The defense patterns that children adopt are learned during the preschool years. They are learned through imitation and seeing what works. These defense mechanisms affect the way they handle anger throughout their adult lives.

It is important to understand that anger in children is normal. It can even be a motivation. As one fourteen-year-old girl explained:

"For me, I have always found anger is motivating. When I had conflicts with one teacher in school, I found it just made me more determined than ever to show him I could do it. If someone tells me I can't do something, it motivates me to say, 'Oh, yes, I can.' And in ninety-nine percent of cases, I do."

While anger can be positive, it can be extremely harmful if misdirected. When turned inward, anger becomes depression. Depression in children is dangerous and requires treatment.

Janice, a nineteen-year-old part-time actress, told how her anger led into a long, childhood depression:

"In middle-class families like ours—my father is a state senator—it seems that problems are hidden or passed over. But you see the results. My sister is thirty and has been divorced twice. I had a serious weight problem.

"I still have a lot of anger at my father. He'd bribe me with presents to lose weight. He was always after me. But I felt it was for him, not me. It was because of his own embarrassment.

"My whole life he's played things that I do *down*, not up. But I never vented my anger at my father. I couldn't. And somehow the anger turned into depression. I can honestly say, I cried from age thirteen to nineteen."

At a 1981 meeting of the American Psychiatric Association, studies by psychiatrists from Children's Hospital National Medical Center in Washington showed that childhood depression can often herald adult depression. Of twelve depressed children studied, only two of the twelve were free of psychopathology three to five years after initially diagnosed.

Yet a control group of symptom-free children on initial evaluation continued to be free of psychopathology on follow-up years later. The study noted that over half of the initially depressed children retained their depression, which usually became chronic. The remainder developed a variety of non-depressive emotional disorders. As these psychiatrists concluded, "Because of the consistency over time of the psychopathology, it seems of paramount importance that childhood depression be taken with utmost seriousness and be vigorously treated."

Depression in children is often due to a depression in the mother. While the conventional thinking had always been, "Anger held in equals depression," Myrna Weissman and Eugene Paykel, in their landmark book *The Depressed Woman*, state that this is too simple. Depressed women are overtly angry and hostile to their children.

Unfortunately, no discussion of anger in women is complete

without mentioning child abuse. For centuries, society implied that by pregnancy and childbirth women were automatically instilled with positive feelings for their children. Within the last twenty years, however, there has been an awareness of child abuse and neglect caused by mothers themselves.

Indeed, the main object of women's hostility and anger are children even more than a spouse. This is because hostile actions towards a husband are tempered out of fear. Women are less fearful of their children. So their unexpressed rage at their spouse becomes directed at a dependent and vulnerable child.

Child abuse is seventy-five percent more common in women than men: 7.2 percent of all mothers but only one percent of all fathers abuse their children. Studies show abuse is perpetrated mainly by mothers of young children because of their own deficient personalities, ambivalent circumstances, or problems innate in the child.

Why is one child singled out for abuse? Studies show an unwanted child is often a victim of abuse. (The stress such a child creates also increases the likelihood of abuse.) A child conceived before the marriage, an unexpected child born very soon after the birth of an older sibling, or a child who taxed the financial resources of the family would be a likely target. Very often, the abused child resembles in personality a disliked spouse. "My sister Janice was always my mother's victim," a twenty-eight-year-old nurse explained. "She'd always say, you are just like your father. Sometimes she would pick on my sister Arlene but Arlene wouldn't take it. She'd scream right back. Janice was more passive."

Interestingly, treatment programs based on "curing" the pathology of the violent person have had only minimal success. Research conducted by Berkeley Planning Associates (1978) on child abuse treatment programs funded by the Federal Government found that, in terms of preventing further abuse, individual counseling was somewhat effective; lay therapy and self-help groups such as Parents Anonymous proved the most effective.

Being a parent, as Sigmund Freud once remarked, is an impossible profession even under the best of circumstances. As a mother of two, I know anger solutions are extremely difficult. Telling what to do is easy but really getting rid of the angry feeling is another matter.

The trouble is that anger causes more anger. You need to feel understood in order to dissolve anger. You can shout at your child all morning but if you don't feel your message has been understood, you will remain tense and angry.

For small angers, a straight physical outlet is good. Walking fast, running, jogging (or for that matter, any sport), hitting your bed with a rolled up towel or just screaming in a closed car can all be useful. For bigger problems, here are some suggestions that may be helpful.

WHAT CHILDREN WANT: To diminish conflict and anger, I asked some children what *they* thought their parents should do. Here are their replies.

Accept me as I am, not as you want me to be. "My parents always tell me how they want me to be, what they want to make me. They can't accept me as I am," one fourteen-year-old explained. "They always have certain things they want you to do. They impose their standards, and there is no room for another side. I can always see both sides of almost any issue. Why can't they?"

Be supportive. "What I found that helped me a lot," one camp counselor explained, "was that my mother was very supportive. She was interested. She would listen. She really couldn't do anything to help but she was always interested. And she was a sounding board. I could vent my feelings freely.

Somehow it made it easier for me to straighten things out in my own mind."

Don't lecture. All children mentioned that lectures—being talked at—were anger provoking and solved nothing.

When children try our patience, many mothers say, "Don't you see how hard I work, etc., etc.," ending with, "So I don't want to hear nonsense like that ever again and don't talk back to me." The sermon is designed to steamroll over the child's opinion, belittle it, imply that it is a stupid opinion and induce guilt. The lecture prevents a real discussion of the underlying problem and therefore never works.

Don't belittle problems. One college student and the youngest of five children related a typical family incident.

"We all went out to dinner. My older sisters were talking about their marriage problems, divorce problems, problems with their children. When I was very quiet, they asked what was bothering me. I said I was very concerned about my courses next year, I wasn't sure what my major should be. My mother said, 'Oh, you're so silly. Why are you worrying about that?' They made me feel very young, as if what I was saying was unimportant and silly. But these things weren't insignificant to me. They really concerned me. It infuriated me."

ADVICE FROM MOTHERS THEMSELVES: "I scream a lot," was the answer most mothers gave to the question "How do you deal with anger at your children?" No one need remind us that exploding isn't always the wisest course. It alienates people, especially children. Dr. Gerd H. Franchel, Dean of the Washington Square Institute, a middle-income treatment center in New York, points out, however, that the person who explodes is better off than the person who sits and broods. Listening is the key to most problem solving. The trouble is most of us do not really listen. We try to overwhelm.

Don't save it up. "I take care of things instantly," one mother of an eight-year-old boy explained. "I find if I say what I think right away, it clears the air immediately. I'll let it out and when it's over, it's behind me like a wave in the ocean that is over and past me."

A mother of three did not use this method, explaining, "If I let out all my anger, I'd constantly be starting fights. It probably would not do any good anyway—and it might do a lot of harm." Psychological studies show, however, that while momentarily it may be more upsetting, expressing feelings prevents tensions. In an open and free home, even one with yelling, there is less anger.

Stop a moment. "Sometimes it helps to stop for a few minutes and ask yourself at what or at whom you're really angry. Just trying to be clear on this has helped me avoid otherwise certain storms," one working mother of three adolescents explained. Although we might be aware that it is not really the children but the frustration at the office that is causing our rage, it still needs to come out. Just the moment of stopping makes you better able to put things in perspective and perhaps not use your children as scapegoats.

If our anger *is,* however, due to the children, don't wait too long. Telling someone how we feel loses effect as time goes on. Timing is very important in getting our real anger over with. The most "relieving" messages are delivered close to the time we get angry.

In therapy, many women notice a timing change in their anger more than anything else. There is a shorter time lapse between the occurrence of an irritating event, a feeling of anger, and a responding verbal message.

Make a special comforting place. A fifty-two-year-old woman said she devised this when her two children, now in professional school, were young. "There was a rocking chair in my son's room. It was our consolation chair when he was little,

I would hold him in my lap and we'd rock. One day I came home—he was only about six—he was rocking away and talking angrily about something that happened in school. Just knowing there was a comfortable place seemed to make him feel better."

Apologize if you get mad at them. A mother of two and now a grandmother offered this suggestion. She said, "I never thought of my children as kids. I thought of them as people. If I got mad and yelled at them, even when they were very, very young, I always would apologize. I felt they deserved it."

Plan in advance. This was the advice of Roanna Shorofsky, director of the esteemed 92nd Street Nursery School in New York City and herself a mother of two.

> "Especially with young children, try to plan ahead. You can organize to avoid anger-inducing situations. For example, if your child is a morning slow-poke, put out his clothes the night before, buy him an alarm clock, and try to prevent the situation."

Talk to the teacher. "I always get angry about things that are avoidable," a mother of three grown children explained. "For example, when my oldest child was in the first grade, I'd ask each day, 'How was school?' He always said, 'Great, wonderful.' In November at my first parent teacher conference, the teacher gave an awful report. He was not cooperative in class; he had never done his homework. I was furious at the teacher. Why didn't she tell me? Why did she wait so long? For my next kids, I always kept in close touch with the teacher. It avoided a lot of anger."

Give real attention. One female psychiatrist explained, "If you give kids what they need *when* they are young, they won't always be after you and always demanding. The mothers who run during the early years give the children a feeling of insecurity and abandonment. These women may find the more they 'run' the more the children will be on their heels."

Spend adequate time. In dealing with children, quality versus quantity of time is always an issue. One psychiatrist who directs a mothering center in Greenwich, Connecticut, and is herself a mother recommended *quantity* without question. She explained, "If I give a starving man the choicest one ounce of filet mignon in the world, he might still starve. Wouldn't it be better if I gave him six or eight ounces, even if it wasn't the choicest meat of all? It is the same with children."

Talk to other mothers. One mother of three children, all under the age of six, said,

"I feel a lot of anger at my husband because of what I have to put up with from the kids. He gets up and goes to work. When he comes home and I blow up at a little thing, he looks at me as if I have fourteen heads. He gives me this 'are you crazy' look. He left his work situation, bad as it might be, behind. He just doesn't understand what it's like being with kids, and in the house all day long. He feels he should come back to a house that 'runs.' With three kids, I can't manage it. His answer is always— no matter how bad you think you have it, you should see what I have to put up with at the office. So what can I say?"

Most men do *not* understand what it is like handling young children continuously. Talking with other mothers will usually produce more real understanding and empathy. It can soothe raw nerves and prevent issues from accumulating to an overflowing emotional level.

"How can we, as mothers, best handle anger at our children?" I asked Dr. Andrew Looker, a child psychiatrist at New York Hospital-Cornell University School of Medicine in New York City. Here are his thoughts:

"First and foremost, mothers must understand it is perfectly okay to be angry, very angry at your children. It is perfectly normal to even hate your children at times. You probably hate them with the same intensity as you love them. This anger is part of a normal loving relationship. It is when we try to deny this anger and hate that destructive patterns begin.

"A lot of parents feel it's wrong to be angry with their children. They feel guilty about their anger and so they try to hide it. The greatest harm is done to our children when we try to 'protect' them from our angry feelings.

"It is perfectly all right to tell a child you are angry at him. You may say, 'You are making me angry,' or even, 'I don't like being with you when you are like this and you probably feel the same way about me sometimes.' Indeed the only thing you should *not* say is 'I am not angry at you' when you are angry.

"Many people erroneously think that child psychiatrists are looking for a single traumatic event in a child's life. A parent's death, divorce, or serious illnesses all present difficulties, but a single trauma is usually not the answer to emotional problems in children. It is chronic patterns and chronic attitudes that cause the real difficulties. These chronic patterns which recur over and over are sometimes due to the fact that a parent won't honestly express her anger forthrightly. So it goes on and on. Emotional damage to the child results.

"Let's talk for a moment about spanking. When a mother is angry, her impulse may be to hit the child. It is easy to strike out in anger. Then the mother feels guilty. A single spanking can do little harm. It is when spanking becomes chronic that difficulties arise.

"The times when mothers and children have most difficulty with anger is during the pre-school period (up to age six) and adolescence (ages eleven to sixteen, with eleven to fourteen being particularly difficult).

"Young babies are charming and appealing but their extreme needs can cause tremendous anger in a mother. It is important to be aware of how angry a baby can make you. This is perfectly normal.

"A lot of new mothers find it difficult to admit to hostility toward their baby. The myth is that a mother should be all loving. It is very difficult to be all loving twenty-four hours a day. That is not the way life is. Even the song 'Rock-A-Bye Baby' contains a lot of hidden hostility toward the baby.

"When a young child becomes angry, it is best to try to have the child express his anger in an undestructive way such as with a punching bag or bobo doll. You can even say directly, 'I see you are angry at me. Why don't you stop yelling and hit this doll.' It is always important to provide substitutes. Say 'Stop this and do this instead....' Dos should always be provided along with the don'ts.

"Adolescence is a time when children struggle for independence and mothers often struggle with intense anger. Bickering is the rule. Moderate bickering is nothing to be concerned about but continual bickering can cause a great deal of anger. There are some things mothers can do so they are not always retaliating. The most important is to set limits.

"It is often better for the parents not to endlessly explain. Saying, 'This is what I believe,' or 'I am your mother and I said so' is enough. While children may be demanding new freedoms, they are really asking for limits.

"What are realistic limits? In our rapidly changing world, some parents feel guilty because they are 'old-fashioned.' It is best not to try to be 'modern.' It is best to trust your instincts and your own behavior code. When parents are not secure in their beliefs and limits are not firm, this is fertile ground for mothers to become very angry. Firmness is essential. All children need things to rebel against.

"While these are general comments and approaches vary depending on the age of the child, it is well to remember that seeking professional help can sometimes be very helpful in dealing with children. By remembering it is okay to be angry, very angry at your children, you will make life easier for yourself and your child too."

Children are continually struggling with dependency, autonomy, and mastery; mothers are constantly juggling anxiety, guilt, and the pressures of the outside world. No wonder anger often occurs.

Learning to deal with anger is, however, most crucial for ourselves as well as our children. If we have difficulties expressing our own emotions honestly, our children most certainly will be doomed to a similar fate. For their sense of well-being as well as our own, our home should be a place where all feelings—the nice and not-so-nice—are openly expressed.

8

Women Working and Overworking

Today over half of all women work. Balancing the demands of a job, a husband, and children is very difficult; at times, we may feel it is impossible. "The main thing that blocks my getting ahead is that it takes all my energy just to stay even," a real estate agent and mother of three told us. A divorced lawyer and mother of two explained, "It's like I have my very small finger in a large overflowing dike."

What are most working women today really feeling? Here are the thoughts of several we interviewed.

Judy Talbot, M.D., a petite and attractive thirty-four-year old woman, is a pediatric endocrinologist. She has been married for a year and works in a large metropolitan hospital.

"It's hard to pinpoint exactly what makes me angry. But most of my anger deals with work.

"I get up at six a.m. for work. Then I see the tinfoil from last night's dinner rolled up in the stove and the chicken fat is still next to the stove. As I make coffee, I feel like I haven't finished last night's supper and it's breakfast already.

"My husband says I have no reason to get angry. I should feel lucky because he's so supportive. But when I see all this, I can't start the morning in a peaceful mood. It's low-grade anger but it's not easily forgotten.

"Then I go to work. I'm dressed in a white coat. But patients don't seem to recognize me as a doctor. A woman patient will say, 'Can I have a male doctor?' Over and over, it seems that women are knocking down other women. I think a large part of my anger comes from other women. There is a female prejudice against women doctors. I feel a definite lack of respect and that gets me angry. Somehow the male doctors command respect, just by being a male.

"Because I'm in pediatrics and am younger than many of the mothers, they have this attitude, 'How can she tell me how to handle my child?' The *coup de grâce* is when they start looking me over head to toe. I feel helpless.

"The secretary in our office gets coffee and a white coat for the male doctor. She doesn't even mind. But she never ever does it for me.

"When I come home I'd like to say I feel relief but I must admit I don't. I'd love to have a dog or a room full of children to come home to. I wish I didn't care about all these things—the woman who looked me up and down, the aluminum foil in the sink, or not having children greet me at the door, but I do care. That's why I'm angry."

Heddy Lemmer has a serenity that instantly draws you to her. Raised in Johannesburg, South Africa, she has been married twelve years, has no children, and worked as a newspaper editor.

"I was trained as a teacher in Johannesburg. Like all my

friends, I was taught that a woman must have something to fall back on. This idea prevails here, but it also prevailed in South Africa. We were taught a woman should get married, have babies, cook dinner, and have teaching if needed.

"I decided at age twenty-three I didn't want children—ever. I didn't want to be like my mother. The most important thing to her were her children—even more than her husband. Even when I was very young, I was conscious of my mother's unhappiness. I thought this stemmed from being so tied down. I was determined to be a wild, free spirit. I was going to read great books, write great books.

"I taught for ten years. After five years, I hated it. The last five years were *very* long. For three years, I couldn't get out of bed in the morning.

"At the beginning, teaching wasn't bad. I worked ten a.m. to two p.m. My biggest class had ten children. But after a few years, I couldn't stand it. The other teachers were unstimulating. It was very isolated and isolating, being with adolescents all day.

"Why did I stay? I think I had a crisis in confidence. I was scared. I really wanted to write so I went to publishers. But I was rejected down the line, over and over. All they offered was typing. I couldn't type and I felt too good to learn.

"Most of all, I believed the rejections. I didn't have the confidence, the ego. I was insecure. I became withdrawn. I thought they were right to reject me. I really believed I was unable to do anything but teach.

"I rationalized. I told myself the usual things: the hours, the pay, the vacations. I told myself teaching would give me time to do my writing. And I did have time: four hours each day. So why didn't I go straight to my desk? I just couldn't. I was beat. Teaching was only four hours but it's draining. And the depression from teaching prevented my doing *anything*.

"I was very angry. Why wasn't I writing when I had the time? Why did I accept a safe paycheck that wasn't good anyway, rather than fight?

"I was angry at myself for not having the guts. But I also got angry at the world. I was sarcastic to my husband. I was always in a foul mood.

"Finally, I've left teaching. I don't have a new job. I have a new life. I should have done it years ago."

Karen Nathanson is forty, tall, blond and works at a leading New York City research firm. In a high-powered management position, she has worked for seventeen years, is married, and has a ten-year-old son.

"My anger is not directed at myself. It is completely work-related. It is mainly towards women at work. My superior is a woman. This is very unusual on my level. There are two women in senior management out of maybe 1,200 men. I'm a Vice President. If there are fifteen women in a position like mine, that's a lot; there are easily 100 men, maybe more.

"You know what I get angry at? I get furious when I see my boss capitulating in a traditional, passive, female way. Here's a perfect example. Six months ago, we were doing a marketing promotion. She gave me some directions and I put a program together. She said it was great, marvelous. During our presentation, however, she saw that the men were questioning some things. She immediately capitulated. She left me completely out on a limb.

"Another time, we were having some trouble on a project. I suggested blending the graphics the agency liked with the visuals the client liked. She vetoed the idea. When a man said the same thing at a meeting she said, 'Great idea.' She never mentioned I had already suggested that and I *know* she remembered.

"She wants me to succeed. But just to a certain level. She doesn't really want me to get too much money or too much success.

"My salary is half of what it should be. She said, 'You can't talk to me every six months about salary.' But I know it would be acceptable if I was a man. I feel *she* is holding me back.

"And then there's the whole sex game—it's okay for men to

flirt at work but it's not okay for women. Even though I'm married, I like to flirt. But I don't feel I can. There is one woman in the office who is attractive and does flirt. The men dismiss her as a lightweight, which is really not true. Women always have to think about how they act but men never do."

Disappointments, ambivalence, frustration and plain exhaustion—all of us encounter such feelings at times. How can we better deal with these emotions? The first step is examining our beliefs about work.

All of us—a young woman first entering the job market, a middle-aged woman re-entering the work force, or a divorced woman needing to support a family—have notions of work. Often these are based on the media. While media presentations are at best incomplete and at worst total fantasy, many of us consciously or subconsciously have absorbed them.

While a few jobs *are* glamorous, these are the exception. As James Barrie put it, "Nothing is really work unless you would rather be doing something else." The truth is most people— women and men alike—do *not* have great jobs. The majority of work is not interesting. It is routine. It does not necessarily provide you with a stimulating few hours. It is what it has always been: a way to earn income. When a job produces little or no sense of accomplishment and many frustrations, however, we feel dissatisfied and angry.

"I knew what I wanted to do—produce educational films," one former programmer explained. "But I could never get one finished and produced. I always had the feeling of grabbing cotton candy. It just wasn't there. I became disillusioned. I lashed out at my husband but nothing changed."

"Good" jobs are demanding and difficult. An attractive, thirty-one-year-old surgeon who just completed her training— four years of college, four years of medical school, six years of surgical residency and one year of fellowship—explained what being a surgeon was really like.

"It's a horrendous life. If I had to do it all over, I would never, never do it again. You have no personal life. It is all consuming, constantly demanding. There is no relief. Every patient that does poorly, you take home with you. I'm always thinking what if this happens, what if that happens, maybe I should have done the other operation....

"It's hard, no impossible, to meet men. I never meet anyone because I'm always working. Of course, I love the work. It's totally fascinating. And doing something so powerful with your own hands, just you and your hands, well, there is nothing else like it."

Women over fifty find the workplace particularly difficult, especially if they have not worked in twenty-five years. Mary Samms, Ph.D., a New York City psychologist, remarked:

"I see many women in their fifties who are very caught by the new standards. They were raised to be wives and mothers. They have maintained fine homes and raised their children. Now they feel they should be allowed to rest on their laurels. Not only is society pressuring them enormously but their husbands are too. One fifty-three-year-old woman poignantly told me, just this morning, 'How can I compete with this thirty-year-old woman executive? She is highly educated and knows as much about the business as my husband. She doesn't have to go home and take care of children and a household. She can be a good mistress. All I can be is a good wife. And John told me, that's not enough anymore.' "

Money is at the root of a great deal of a woman's work anger. The best security—indeed, the only security—is knowing you can earn a good livelihood for yourself. Without this, you are forever dependent on someone else. If you are financially able to face life alone, you won't build up as much anger and resentment.

While poor women have always been overburdened, they may have less anger. They always knew they had to earn their own livelihood; they never felt that they were going to be "taken care of." On the other hand, middle-class women were raised with the idea that first Daddy and then their husband would "take care of them." Many women are ill-equipped to earn their own livelihood.

After a death or divorce, the lifestyle of the woman has the most shocking financial downfall. No woman takes this adjustment well. They become filled with anger. And it lingers, due to the enormous inequities. Emily Jane Goodman, a well-known New York divorce lawyer, cautions that it's not likely a divorced woman can ever earn what her ex-husband does, especially if she's lost ten to twenty years in her career. "That's why I believe that an ex-wife is owed something for the past," she says. "It's just not enough to put her in a position—through schooling, for example—where she becomes self-supporting. Most women I see are not and never will be able to equalize the economics of the situation."

One doctor's wife who worked as a nurse after her divorce commented, "Yes, I work but I have never earned enough to say, 'The hell with you.' Although he has a great deal of money, he doles it out painfully. I am a prisoner of that financial payment."

Today most women must work. The second income is not just wanted, it is actively needed. When a woman does find work she enjoys, it may not pay well. The resulting conflicts were described by a forty-year-old aerobic dance instructor.

"I like teaching aerobics. I felt frustrated not working. The kids are teenagers and I need a goal. But last year, I almost quit.

I was not eating, the house was getting dirty, the kids were difficult to handle. I was overburdened. I tried to be a superwoman—supermom, superwife, superhostess. I got angry when my husband didn't understand but I also felt guilty about my anger.

"The main problem was, I wasn't earning enough money. If it was a job that paid well, it would have been easier asking for compromises from my family. The money, or I should say the lack of it, really caused all the ambiguity. If I was earning a lot, I would not have felt so torn."

Are most women underpaid? According to 1982 statistics compiled by the U.S. Department of Labor, Bureau of Labor Statistics, the answer is unquestionably yes. Overall, full-time women workers make about sixty cents for every dollar earned by men. A three-year study of 50,000 people showed the median weekly earnings of women were much lower than those of men doing essentially the same work. For example, although women held 90.6 percent of the bookkeeping jobs, they earned an average of ninety-eight dollars a week less than men holding the same job.

Among the other earnings comparisons listed in this survey were these:

* Male administrators of elementary and secondary schools earned an average of $520 a week as against $363 for women.
* Although women held 68.5 percent of the health technician jobs in hospitals and clinics, they earned an average weekly wage of $273 against $324 for men.
* Female elementary school teachers earned an average sixty-eight dollars a week less than males, even though women held 82.2 percent of those jobs. Although women and men often make the same entry-level salaries, after a few years men generally make more.

* Although over 50 percent of all women work, less than 5 percent of all managerial positions are held by women. Among executives paid $25,000 and up per year, only 2.3 percent are women. Clerical work (traditionally low-paying) is still the largest and fastest employment area for women.

Not only do women earn less but they have to pay high fees for baby-sitters as well. In a recent article, "Does It Pay a Wife To Get a Job," in *Woman's Day* magazine, the truth about how ridiculously little is left after work-related expenses was illustrated with clarity. A Detroit woman with two pre-school children returned to work as a bookkeeper and sent her children to a day-care center. After deducting expenses, her salary looked like this:

Bookkeeper's Salary	$11,000
Taxes	
Wife's income and Social Security	$ 3,190
Husband's additional	$ 1,650
Transportation and lunches	$ 600
Additional clothing and upkeep	$ 450
Child care	$ 1,500
Actual Net Income	$ 3,610

There are, of course, other compensations besides cash for working. Dr. Mortimer R. Feinberg, Director of Advanced Management Programs and Assistant Dean of Baruch College in New York, explained:

"There are enormous psychological advantages for the woman in the labor force. She feels a sense of competence, she is a more interesting conversationalist, her image of herself is elevated and she learns to organize her time better. She gets dressed up every day and is more attractive at home. She can also better understand the pressures her husband is under on his job."

Money is not the only working woman's problem. After working all day just as hard as a man, many women must then go home to a second job: wife and mother. Are men helping out? Perhaps more than years ago, but studies indicate women are still the main workers inside the home. A March, 1982 survey by *Good Housekeeping* magazine of readers in ten cities showed that only:

one out of six husbands cooks dinner,
one out of twelve husbands does the laundry,
one out of six husbands cleans the house,
one out of three husbands helps with the grocery shopping.

Family relationships are inevitably stressed when a woman works. It is very difficult for women who must be decisive on the job with the same aggressiveness and assertiveness required by men to assume the traditional passive role at home.

To add to the pressures, fatigue is mixed in. After an emotionally draining day at the shop, office or factory, a woman is less giving and more demanding of others. "I always laughed at those cartoons of the man at home who only wanted to sit with his feet up unbothered and read the newspaper," a thirty-four-year-old editor said. "I don't laugh anymore. That's me."

Dr. Jay B. Rohrlich, a New York City psychiatrist and author of *Work and Love,* has identified another work dilemma for women. He became interested in women's reactions to work while listening to the problems of his patients. Although many of them were competent at work, they could not relax enough to enjoy their families, mate or lover.

Dr. Rohrlich attributes this to a work/love paradox. Work and love, he believes, require abilities that are emotionally and intellectually opposite. Work demands control; love asks that we throw control out of the window. In work, we must plan weeks ahead; in love, we must release ourselves to the moment.

This does not mean that combining work and love is impossible. Work gives us the money, time and self-esteem needed to be a good love partner. But some women (as well as men) find it difficult to shift gears from work relationships to a love relationship. This is because some women (and men) use work to compensate for feelings of inadequacy from childhood. They may work compulsively and then are unable to let go in love.

While Dr. Rohrlich sees no simple solutions for this common dilemma, he does believe that examining and understanding our real motivations can help us attain more emotional and professional satisfaction.

At work, we must suppress our angry feelings. So we send signals, some conscious, most unconscious.

Accident-proneness is one such anger signal. We are accident-prone when angry because anger interferes with our natural alertness. Psychiatrists also offer another interpretation. They explain that many of us grow up feeling guilty if we are angry. It follows, then, that if we feel guilty, we deserve some punishment. Wanting to punish ourselves for our anger, we put ourselves in positions where accidents (punishment) can occur.

A woman who feels her boss expects too much and pays too little might express her anger through procrastination—leaving letters untyped and projects uncompleted, allowing files to pile up on her desk. Other anger disguises on the job are perpetual forgetfulness, chronic lateness and lying. All of these stratagems are messages a person uses to convey the resentment, frustration and anger she can not openly express.

At one time or another, we all use such tactics. However, if someone is always angry and incapable of ever communicating openly, these can become self-destructive, chronic patterns. Defined not so much by what you do as what you don't do, the motive is always revenge. The worker does not want to run the risk of confronting her boss, so she seeks revenge against him while still holding onto her job.

The woman president of an international conglomerate who earns $250,000 a year told me, "If I found the right man I'd drop it all and go off in a minute—no, quicker than a minute." Unfortunately, this sentiment is not unusual, even among the most successful women. Few men would say or even contemplate this. To get more real satisfaction from work, some working women offered the following suggestion:

1. *Kick the Old Habits.* This is easy to say but terribly difficult to do. "I knew all the things intellectually," one thirty-seven-year-old single nurse admitted, "but actually, loosening myself from that monthly paycheck was another matter. I was just plain afraid. It was easier to continue along as usual." A teacher-turned-tennis-center-manager explained, "I rationalized, reciting all the advantages—money, convenience, time, vacations. But these added up to just one thing: security. Leaving my job after ten years was one of the most difficult things I've ever done." If standard tests, such as civil service examinations, are required for a career change, these just increase our tension and anger. Recent studies show that test anxiety is notoriously higher in women than men.

But nothing produces more anger than going to bed at night and dreading getting dressed for work in the morning. While very difficult, psychiatrists say, taking a risk is the answer to much job frustration. You will be much less angry at yourself and others if you try something and it doesn't work than if you regret missed opportunities. From women who did change careers, we heard only one regret over and over, "I waited too long."

2. *Try To Know What You Really Like To Do.* Most

women we interviewed felt this is not something that can be really thought out. It only comes with maturity, with life's experiences. However, people are aware of their own interests. Turning these into satisfying work is the goal. Rationalizing when we are unsure of ourselves and our abilities leads to compromise, dissatisfaction and inevitable anger. Meaningful work, on the other hand, enhances your self-esteem, your entire outlook, even your appearance.

As Christopher Morley wrote, "There is only one success— to be able to spend your life in your own way."

3. *Get Up Fifteen Minutes Earlier.* Most women have too much to do in too short a time. More time will reduce stress and anger levels.

4. *Set Goals.* Goals give a sense of purpose. They greatly reduce frustration, aimlessness and anger. Most of us do not set goals because we are not sure of our wants. In making goals, we must, therefore, first decide for *ourselves* (not our employers, parents, spouses or children)—what *we* really want. Then we should:

Set target dates. A goal doesn't become a goal until you have set a deadline.

Write down the goal. A breakdown into long-range as well as daily goals is helpful.

Publicize the goal. Telling others increases motivation and makes quitting tougher.

Start working at once. Studies show the more quickly you begin a project, the greater the likelihood it will be completed.

5. *Re-Think the Provocation.* By rearranging your thinking, you can view an anger-inducing event less personally. For example, Ray Novaco, who teaches at the University of California at Irvine, believes that anger is fomented and maintained by the statements we make to ourselves—"How could he treat me that way? Who does he think I am?" He teaches

those who have problems with chronic anger how to lessen their anger by re-thinking the situation. He shows how to place the onus on the offender—"She must be an unhappy person," "Only an insecure person would do that..." rather than blaming yourself. (This is what people who are slow to anger do naturally.)

This reappraisal method has been effectively taught to those exposed to provocations on the job. New York City bus drivers, for example, see a film showing how passengers who induce a great deal of anger may actually have hidden handicaps. They learn that repeated questions may indicate uncontrollable and severe anxiety; apparent drunkenness may, in fact, be cerebral palsy; mild epileptic seizures may cause an indifference to orders. One bus driver who saw the film explained his change of attitude. "The film makes you feel funny about the way you've treated passengers in the past. Before I saw this film, if a passenger rang the bell five times, I'd take him five blocks to get even. Now I'll say, 'Maybe the person is sick.' "

6. *Don't Take Any Business Action in Anger.* Try not to say a word until you cool off. At work, emotional outbursts tend to be ignored or *worse.*

Be diplomatic with everyone, not just the boss but co-workers as well. For example, if you asked a co-worker to prepare a report that was done unsatisfactorily, you might say, "George, you obviously spent a great deal of time and work on the report. If you can gather more statistical material, I think we can combine it with this information and come up with a good presentation." A bawling out, given in anger and with sarcasm, usually does not work. The person who feels harmonious towards you will perform better for you. This will not only make them less angry, it will make you less angry and more successful.

While you are not working to win a popularity contest, you

are working to earn money, do well and feel a sense of accomplishment. All of these will have a better chance if you appear confident and not angry. What about an assignment you honestly feel is not going to work? Jo Foxworth, the author of *Wising Up, The Mistakes Women Make in Business and How To Avoid Them,* advises, "The people who are investing their money and/or time, talent and energy in a project like to feel that it's going to work. If you think it won't, say so and say why—but having said it, do all that you can to make it work anyway!"

7. *Know Your Money Needs.* All of us have different priorities in working. We are all interested in salary, but to some it is more crucial. If money is your chief aim, try to move into a better-paying field. (Some occupations traditionally pay more.) According to Thelma Kandel, author of *What Women Earn,* the best-paying professions with the greatest number of new openings per year during the 1980's include accountants (61,000 new jobs a year), engineers (46,500), lawyers (37,000), physicians (19,000) and life scientists (11,200).

Among managerial jobs, the highest-paid and most in demand include bank officials and managers (28,000 new jobs a year), personnel and labor relations workers (17,000) and health service administrators (18,000). Among high-paying blue collar fields, industrial machinery repairers and machinists will be most in demand.

8. *Don't Make an Issue Over a Small Thing.* While a picayune point can make you very angry, in the business world small things are best left unmentioned. If you go along with small points, you will get a more receptive hearing on a big point.

9. *Use Womanly Ways.* Rightly or wrongly, being a woman affects us greatly at work. Rather than constantly fighting this, take advantage of it. One computer programmer said, "I can get much further by being sweet, charming and helpful. The

guys will say, 'Hello, sweetheart,' or some other blatant sexist term but I don't care, I'm always friendly; I always smile. What happens is the manager will say, 'Oh, let Alice try the thing.' I know it is much tougher for the men to get time on the computer. I just smile and get it."

10. *More than Anything, Have Ambition.* I believe—more than intelligence, money or talent—ambition is the secret of success. Perhaps my faith comes from my experience at a large publishing company. Working as an associate editor, I saw excellent manuscripts rejected (we may have been looking for a gardening book and they submitted a book on aerospace). Likewise, I saw mediocre works published. Persevering until one found the right slot seemed the secret.

Jane Trahey, in her book *Women and Power,* states, "If I have a message for women who want power, it's this: Achieving power (especially when you start with nothing but your mother's warning that you are destined to be a great failure) is a combination of timing, luck and hard work. Plus one other ingredient women overlook a lot, that's wanting power."

A friend of mine who designed women's lingerie worked full time as a sales clerk for seven years while designing at night. Over and over, she would say to herself, "Why am I wasting my time?" "It's hopeless." "It's just too tough competing with the big merchandisers." Eventually she was able to support herself but it was not easy.

Lena Horne, culminating her Broadway success on her sixty-fifth birthday, said, "Young people today think it should be easier than it is. We become angry when we fail. We must work not just hard but very, very, very hard to succeed."

Will women's work angers lessen? Unfortunately, more difficulties may be ahead. Hostility in men—both husbands and co-workers—may increase as women compete and get jobs traditionally held by men. With technology erasing the traditional advantages of male size and strength, the sexes are now equal when it comes to pushing a button. Dealing with feelings, especially anger, in the workplace may therefore become increasingly important.

9

How Anger Affects Our Bodies

Unexpressed anger not only creates an emotional burden, it produces a physical stress. It can, without doubt, make us physically ill.

Everyone has a special place where they physically feel their unexpressed anger. We all know women who get splitting headaches, or rashes, or a weak stomach, or heart palpitations, or constant colds. Few of us escape. One in ten people develop ulcers; one in five get debilitating headaches; one in six suffer from high blood pressure. Doctors aren't sure why some people react to anger by developing skin problems and others get ulcers. They do know that the way each of us responds to our emotions depends on the genes we've inherited.

The common refrain "I've just got one of my...again" is said instead of "I'd like to kick your teeth in," which is closer to the anger felt. By masking real feelings with physical symptoms, a woman saves herself from being rejected due to her anger. But she does not save her body. The damage is not imagined. It is real and can be severe.

Our emotions and our physical functioning all take place in one body. Doctors know that anger causes immediate physical changes—blood rushing to the face (blushing), quickening heart beat, a strong desire to yell and wave one's arms and hands.

The long-term body effects of anger are more difficult to measure. Does it make us more susceptible to viral infections? Can it cause malignant disease? Is prevention possible through a change in attitude? To better understand the answers to these and other questions let's start with some myths about anger and illness.

Psychosomatic ailments are not "all in your head." While hypochondria is an imagined illness, psychosomatic illnesses cause actual bodily malfunctions which the doctor can detect and diagnose. A psychosomatic illness is one caused by or greatly influenced by our emotions.

People who suffer psychosomatic illnesses do not "want" to be sick. They are not malingerers, people who fake an illness and know it. These people consciously, even subconsciously, want to get well.

Dr. Raymond Simon, a New York City internist with an interest in emotional disease, told us that women tend to somatize much more than men and consequently visit the physician more frequently. He estimates about a three to one female-male ratio. "A lot of women come in with the classic psychodynamic aspects of anger—primarily depression. I see many women in their forties and fifties with many vague symptoms that never seem to get better. They don't feel fulfilled. They feel unable to change things and they are angry at this helplessness. Sometimes they complain of muscle spasm in their neck or back but I can find no demonstrable physical pathology. Often they say they don't feel rested at the end of a night's sleep. Interestingly, their symptoms will improve with anti-depressants while muscle relaxants don't make them feel any better."

Do these women talk about their anger? "When they somatize," Dr. Simon explained, "they don't talk about their anger. If I draw them out by asking, 'Have you been upset recently?' 'Is something bothering you?' sometimes they will express anger but they don't connect the two. They will strongly deny that their physical complaints could be due to their anger."

If you are *always* tired—not a little tired, but constantly, chronically fatigued—the reason is probably not anemia or hypoglycemia. It may be anger.

Muscles are particularly affected by anger. People who are angry may use their entire bodies to ward off anger or any show of it. They go around in a constant state of muscular tension. It is almost as if their bodies are kept physically on guard in a semi-contracted state lest any anger show.

Of course, this is completely subconscious. We are not aware we are doing it. However, our body feels the pressure. Fatigue results. Such fatigue is not just imagined. It is very real indeed.

How does the anger-body response work? Our autonomic nervous system, the nervous system not under our voluntary control, regulates the functioning of all our body organs. It has two parts. One, called the parasympathetic system, maintains the everyday operations and any recuperative processes that are needed. The other, the *sympathetic nervous system*, goes into emergency operation when a sudden unusual demand is made on our body.

When we get angry, our body, and specifically our sympathetic nervous system, prepares for action. More sugar pours into our blood so we have more energy. Our blood circulates faster, increasing blood pressure and making the heart beat faster. More adrenalin is secreted, dilating the pupils of the eyes so we see better. If our body remains "on alert," however, this causes harm.

Why would our body stay "on alert?" Let's look at two examples. If a car suddenly comes off the road towards us, our body signals danger and we jump out of the way. After the car passes, our alert system turns back to normal. Our body goes on alert and off again quickly and efficiently. On the other hand, if we dislike our boss and feel he may fire us, our body goes on alert. But our job and our feelings of anger at our boss may continue for years. Because there is no resolution, our body may stay on alert.

Since all of us have things which make us tense and angry, why does one person develop physical symptoms and another stay perfectly healthy? Doctors say it is not the event itself, but the way we handle the resulting anger that determines if physical damage will result.

"Sometimes people deny their anger but you can tell," Dr. Anna Burton, a New Jersey psychiatrist, explained. Angry people look angry: It shows in their faces. Pinched-together eyebrows, scowling without realizing it and a tense tight look are all signs of the anger we so desperately want to hide.

Anger looks different than anxiety. Dr. Burton explained, "You can see it in the resting expression of the face. You can definitely see it. Sometimes anger is very apparent: a facial grimace, waving arms, pointing finger, raised voice. Or it may be more subtle: a change of stance, a lowering of the eyes, a frown or sulk. An angry person will tell a story and in the dramatic telling I, as a listener, will begin to feel myself getting angry. She shows me the anger. She slips me the queen without even realizing it."

Many over-tense, over-angry people clench their teeth without realizing it. It is almost as if they were so fearful lest the truth get out, they keep their jaws subconsciously on guard at all times. This can cause pain in the neck or jaw or ringing in the ears.

Sometimes people who are angry bite their lips; others may clench their fists almost in a punching position.

Dermatologists say many skin conditions are caused by anger. Skin temperature drops when you're angry. Even if we try to hide our anger, our skin reflects how we really feel. We blush with embarrassment, sweat when fearful and get gooseflesh from terror. Anger shows in many ways: redness, hives, acne, even itching.

"I'd get hives on my face," a twenty-five-year-old model explained. "If I was really upset, my entire face would break out in welts. It would last one to two hours. My face would get beet red. I couldn't do anything about it. I'd try to cover it with pimple cream but it never really worked.

"It was always due to a bad interaction with a guy I was dating. It was always related to a man, never a woman. It was always something cruel he had said or done.

"What did I do? I would get in my car and drive very fast. I'd open the two windows in front and let the wind go through my hair. It made me feel better. Now that I think of it, it's a miracle I never killed anyone. I had no concern about myself or others. I just wanted to go—and fast."

Hives, a common symptom of repressed anger, are caused by the leaking of serum—a component of blood—into the skin. This happens when the blood vessels are stimulated by histamine, a body chemical contained in cells that circulate under the skin. These cells release histamine for a number of reasons—allergic response is probably the most common. However, some people have skin cells with membranes so sensitive that the slightest pressure or even exposure to sun or cold will cause the release of histamine. Other people's skin cells are so sensitive to changes in the levels of specific hormones and chemicals that emotional stress causes eruptions.

Acne can also be anger-related. There are 20,000 oil glands (dermatologists call them sebaceous glands) in the face. Oil secreted by these glands comes up a canal that connects the gland to the pore opening on the surface of the skin. Acne occurs when the oil can't escape; it hardens beneath the surface of the skin and forms a plug, which blocks the flow of the remaining oil. As the oil builds up, the gland swells. A pimple results. Changes in hormone levels and other emotional factors can stimulate an increased production of oil.

Psoriasis and eczema are both hereditary skin conditions, but they can be aggravated by anger—a fight with your mother or a bad day at work, for instance. Patches of psoriasis—dry, red, thickened areas of skin covered with silvery scales— typically appear on the elbows, knees, scalp and, occasionally, the nails, and they sometimes itch. A very common type of eczema, atopic dermatitis, often flares up in the folds of the elbows and knees, scalp, upper arms and back, face and fingers or toes. Atopic dermatitis leaves the skin red, thickened, dry and extremely itchy.

Itching, a condition doctors call pruritus, is another anger-related condition. Even the expression "I'm itching to get my hands on him" reflects the connection between our outer covering and our inner feelings. One female form of pruritus which is especially uncomfortable is the itching around the female genitalis called pruritus vulva.

NOTE: For any rash, even one caused by emotions, you should consult a dermatologist. A visit to a dermatologist is important because skin eruptions can cause a break in the skin, exposing the body to infection.

One forty-two-year-old automotive executive described her feelings and her resulting physical problems this way:

"I'm a little overwrought now. When that last relationship ended, it was just 'it' for me. I'm forty-two and still single. I've had so many relationships end, I just cannot take it anymore. When I feel like this, it is not that apparent at work or with my friends. What I think happens is my responses become exaggerated. A minor upset suddenly becomes a major event. It's enough to give me a headache.

"My headaches start between my right eyebrow and the top row of my teeth, on my right side. They last one day. I wake up with them and there is nothing I can do until they go away.

"Well, there is one thing, just one, that sometimes works. If I can turn my mind to some object outside myself and stop dwelling on myself and my own stuff, it will go away but I can't always do that."

A secretary who is studying acting told me:

"My headache was always right behind my forehead. it pounded back and forth. It lasted for hours. It lasted until the reason for my annoyance was removed. Since it took a very long time before I got the courage to say something, I would really suffer. Sometimes I would put a cold compress on my forehead and that helped a little."

The commonest complaint of all to doctors is headache. Few people have never suffered a headache and many people's lives are made completely miserable by a chronic headache. Women most prone to anger—those with tremendous pressure at work or home or high-achiever types who pressure themselves—are also those most prone to headaches. Even our language links headaches with repressed anger. We speak of "blowing my stack," "letting off steam," or "a pain in the neck."

Many women—statistics say twenty percent of the population—suffer headaches. (About eighty percent of all headaches are due to tension. Unexpressed anger is often the underlying cause of tension.) One woman admitted she never actually gets a headache but automatically says, "My head is killing me," when she is angry. Another said, when faced with an anger-inducing situation, she is usually able to handle it calmly. The next day, however, she is certain to have a severe headache.

Anger headaches are due to a tightening of the muscles surrounding the skull. They may feel like a very tight skullcap or a band around the head which is being squeezed. The pains often go down the back of the neck.

"I walk around with headaches and I hold my husband personally responsible," a mother of four explained. "It is totally because of George my head hurts. He places tremendous pressure on me."

Sometimes migraine headaches, which are more serious and disabling, can also be due to repressed anger.

Migraine headaches are more common in women. The ratio of women to men sufferers is about seven to one. Migraines occur when the blood vessels of the head expand and pulsate. These headaches are also related to the menstrual period, estrogen therapy or a family history of such headaches. A classic migraine is characterized by nausea, vomiting and a sensitivity to sound and light. Such headaches usually occur on only one side of the brain. They last between twelve and twenty-four hours and are very painful.

Chronic migraine sufferers are often warned of an oncoming attack by seeing an "aura"—hazy blue light—or spots before their eyes. This may be due to blood vessel spasm, which sometimes precedes the dilation of the blood vessels.

The female hormone estrogen, which causes the blood vessels to expand, may be associated with migraines in women. Many sufferers say the headaches occur during their menstrual cycle (a time of high estrogen production) and cease after menopause (a time of low estrogen). The estrogen in oral contraceptives also explains why many women suffer headaches as a side effect of the pill.

For the generalized dull pain of a tension headache, the usual remedy is to take two aspirins (or over-the-counter equivalent if your stomach won't tolerate aspirin), lie down in a dark quiet place and relax until the ache goes away—usually an hour or so.

Drugs called vasoconstrictors, which contract the blood vessels, are helpful to some migraine sufferers. Interestingly, certain foods and drinks which are known as vasodilators (these help expand the blood vessels) can bring on migraines in susceptible people. Such foods include delicatessen meats treated with nitrates (bologna, frankfurters); red wine; smoked, pickled, or fermented food (pungent cheese, for example); and sometimes nuts and chocolate.

Be Aware: Headaches caused by chronic anger usually respond to reassurance, relaxation techniques or simple aspirin. However, headaches may be due to organic problems— allergies, meningitis, brain tumor, hemorrhages, and eye strain.

If you are troubled by persistent headaches, you should consult a physician. It is important to tell a doctor about any headache that recurs persistently, even if it is successfully treated with aspirin.

A dull, throbbing headache in the back of the head, occurring most often in the morning, may indicate high blood pressure. If you suffer from this kind of headache, and even if aspirin relieves it, you must have your blood pressure checked. A drug called propranolol hydrochloride—its trade name is inderal—is widely used in the control of hypertension because it acts as a vascoconstrictor.

A Suggestion: Sometimes biofeedback techniques can teach a person to control the skull muscles and thereby relieve headaches. For unknown reasons, however, this technique provides relief only in certain cases. A physician is best qualified to recommend a certified biofeedback therapist.

In biofeedback, a biological signal such as a quickened pulse or muscle tightening is electronically amplified and played to the person. By watching these electronic signals, a person learns, through practice, how to control processes of the autonomic nervous system formerly considered beyond conscious manipulation. The best results have been with migraine patients who learn to raise their head temperature. By so doing, blood to the head is diminished and the attack does not occur. Interestingly, biofeedback has been successful in reducing menstrual pain by increasing blood flow to the uterus.

Gastrointestinal problems may also be a manifestation of anger. The way your stomach reacts when you are angry is the same way it reacts when you ingest something toxic—it hurts. People who swallow their anger are particularly prone to diseases of the gastointestinal tract, a thirty-foot-long system extending from the mouth to the rectum. They frequently get cramps and nauseousness and begin vomiting for the "slightest reason."

"I was belching and hiccupping constantly," a forty-five-year-old woman who has been legally separated for two years explained. "I went for an upper GI series. When the doctor came in to talk to me, he said, 'Do you know my diagnosis? There's a lot of terrific women out there but there's not a lot of nice men out there.' It was a sweet thing to say. It comforted me."

Peptic ulcers and chronic indigestion (often a precursor of ulcers) are well-known anger-related problems. Of course, anyone can get peptic ulcers—even babies. No one knows precisely what produces these sores in the stomach or small intestine but bottling in feelings is known to play a part.

Shelly, a twenty-four-year-old divorcée who was still enraged at her "ex," gave us almost a textbook description:

"It was above my stomach right between my breasts. Any time I had any anxiety, it would start to hurt. It was a constant burning that just wouldn't stop. It would go on for hours. It was more or less intense depending on the anxiety. I couldn't eat anything. I had no appetite. I couldn't drink at all. If I drank, I'd get sick. The only thing I wanted was yogurt. Sometimes I had to go to bed, it was so incapacitating. Finally, I went to the doctor and he told me I had a pre-ulcer condition. He gave me Librex pills, I took them three times a day. They helped, but I realized I just had to take a look at myself. I knew I was very mad. I was furious. But I never said anything. I always held it inside me."

There are many theories about the causes of ulcers. One psychological interpretation is that the person who develops a gastric ulcer is basically dependent and wants to be mothered. However, she finds these dependency wishes repulsive and becomes angry at herself for wanting to be cared for like a baby. It is fascinating that the traditional cure for ulcers—milk and cream—is actually the diet of a baby.

Obstetricians tell us that pregnant women who experience "morning sickness" may have an unconscious anger at being pregnant and wish to rid themselves of the child. But this is emotionally unacceptable so the woman changes it subconsciously into a more "acceptable" form.

What can you do about such problems? First and foremost, a doctor must be consulted since stomach problems can have serious complications. You may also want to try deep breathing exercises. If you inhale slowly and deeply, you will begin to exhale some anger and tension. Try this simple exercise which can even be done at your desk at work. Sit down, relax and take long, deep, slow breaths, breathing in through the nose to a count of three and out through the mouth to the count of four. If you are still troubled, perhaps the advice of Leroy (Satchel) Paige, one of the folk heroes of baseball's old Negro leagues, will work. He advised, "If your stomach disputes you, lie down and pacify it with some cool thoughts."

For years, gynecologists and women themselves believed a woman was to blame if her emotional symptoms were not easily traced or cured. Indeed, those without these symptoms believed themselves "more normal," thus superior to women with these emotions.

Today scientists have physical evidence that these women are not neurotic but may have a problem called *premenstrual syndrome*. Premenstrual syndrome, a hormonally related problem, can cause true temporary disability. Anger is another side effect.

Sally Feld, a pretty college junior and skilled horsewoman explained:

> "I become angriest and most disgusted with everyone and everything several days, sometimes a week, before my period. My body aches, I feel tired and drained of energy. I'm in a terrible mood. My anger is usually vented in a bitchy attitude towards friends, my boyfriend, school, and just about anything I can lay my hands on. I once even flew into a rage because the lock got stuck on my front door. All this moodiness and anger lasts exactly six days. Once I get my period it goes away. It's been this way since my period began. Everyone says physical performance isn't affected by the menstrual cycle, but I don't believe it. Any track meet, dance class, or horse show that fell right before my period were ones in which my performance was substandard. I also made more mistakes when I worked at the bank on the days before my period."

Katharina Dalton, a London-based gynecologist-endocrinologist who has been working with these patients since 1948, first used the term *premenstrual syndrome*. She explained, "Characteristically, patients with premenstrual syndrome have more than one symptom. Apart from tension, sufferers from premenstrual migraine (for example) may also complain of premenstrual abdominal bloating, backache, weight gain, constipation, acne, headaches, lethargy, cravings for sweet or salty foods, and breast tenderness."

Modern women have fewer children and therefore more menstrual periods than centuries ago. Does this doom us to even more premenstrual tension? It is difficult to say since doctors still do not know the cause of this problem. Some believe PMS is caused by hormonal imbalance; others say it is due to the retention of salt and water. Poor diet, lack of adequate exercise, and mineral deficiencies also may be contributing factors.

There are several currently recommended treatments. One is exercise. In 1971 two Scandinavian scientists did a study of the menstrual experiences of competitive athletes and gymnasts. They found that athletics had a strikingly favorable effect on the premenstrual syndrome, while inactivity contributed to the severity of premenstrual symptoms.

Dr. Dalton believes that premenstrual syndrome is due to a hormone imbalance in which there is too little progesterone in relation to estrogen. She reports that when pure progesterone is used (the synthetics, although cheaper, do not always work), the remission of symptoms is nearly one hundred percent.

Other physicians believe premenstrual syndrome is due entirely to water retention, a result of salt being retained in the cells and thereby attracting and holding water. Interestingly, doctors say that irritability can result from the response of nerve cells to an imbalance of sodium and potassium due to an excess of sodium. To control water retention, doctors tell women to avoid high salt foods, and not to add salt in cooking or at the table during the week before their period. In most cases, this alone works. If water retention continues, however, diuretics (pills which flush excess water out of the system) can be prescribed.

If you feel angry and irritable before your period, you may find one of these methods, or several combined, will lessen the emotional intensity.

Another area affected by anger is the colon. Diarrhea and constipation are often manifestations of anger. A child may express anger by getting diarrhea, thereby forcing the parent to clean him up. Or he may develop constipation, perhaps an unconscious wish to keep anger—foul matter—inside.

"My stomach acts up in two ways," a forty-year-old woman who has suffered a spastic colon since college explained. "Either I eat something—Mexican food, too many french fries, too much salad, an overload of fat or oil, milk, apple juice or hot spices—or I am feeling very tense about a problem. I associate anger with tension because whenever I'm tense, I also feel very angry. For me, it's hard to admit anger because it's an ugly feeling I try to avoid. When I do get the courage to express my anger, though, it's a great release."

While she felt her problem was partly genetic (both her parents were sufferers), and sometimes "the runs" came for no apparent reason, this woman had found few cures. She told me, "I take Lomotil, an immensely effective medicine with few side effects. My Daddy, an old-fashioned G.P., used to say, 'Rub your belly and be nice to it.' Sometimes this self-soothing helps but the most reliable thing, I find, is these pills."

Doctors say nearly all of us have experienced colon symptoms when emotionally angry and upset. One young actress admits she gets cramps the day before an audition. A middle-aged writer told us she always suffers cramps and diarrhea for about a week after finishing a short story. Other symptoms include: a sore abdomen, diarrhea (often around breakfast time, sometimes followed by constipation), loss of appetite but no weight loss, vomiting, headaches, fatigue and mucus in the stool.

Diseases of the colon may be due to the fact that your colon, which is constantly contracting and relaxing, reacts to the anger you feel and changes its rhythm. If nerve impulses to your intestine are too strong, a spasm results.

One of the best ways of reducing such destructive anger is to recognize that there are millions of "want tos" and "have tos" and "should haves" in life. By dividing tasks and events into categories—essential, important and trivial—we can get more perspective on our angers. We must learn to accept a less-than-perfect job. We must focus on the positive parts rather than concentrating on the failures. Of course, this is easier said than done. It takes a continual and conscious effort.

The most common disease of all—the common cold—is probably related to repressed anger. While no one knows the exact cause or cure for a cold, one widely accepted theory states that most people carry cold viruses around in their bodies all the time.

If we are exposed to another person with a cold, we may get an overload of virus sufficient to overwhelm our natural resistance. Or we may lower our resistance through emotional fatigue. (With cold analysis, the viruses that cause the cold are less important than the question of what lowers our resistance.)

Probably a major factor in this emotional fatigue and lowered resistance is anger. Some people even recognize that they develop colds when they are under tremendous emotional strain.

A fascinating study at the Great Lakes Naval Medical Research Unit and Cornell Medical School showed that women were not the only ones susceptible to "angry" colds. A group of men with similar medical status were exposed to "cold" germs. Only those men struggling with feelings of depression, anger and frustration in their personal lives caught colds. The virus had no effect on the others.

One noted psychiatrist told of having patients develop nasal congestion, mucoid discharge, even asthmatic attacks in the middle of talking about an unhappy marriage, anger at parents or how someone had hurt them.

A Commonsense Tip: Despite all the publicity about Vitamin C and megavitamins, the best treatment for the common cold, and the anger beneath it, is still better eating and better sleeping habits. Fatigue can greatly reduce one's ability to cope with anger-inducing situations. By getting enough sleep (sleeping pills prevent restful sleep) and eating regular, well-balanced meals, you will develop a better energy reserve. You will have more emotional as well as physical strength.

Most of us get angry at being sick. Pain causes anger. "What were the feelings of the other patients?" we asked a thirty-three-year-old graduate student who had just suffered his second heart attack. "I saw a tremendous amount of anger on the part of the patients. I couldn't blame them, they'd be nasty to their wives—not want to see them. The women seemed reasonable: they loved their husbands or felt sorry for them—or a little of both."

A wife talking about her husband's hospitalization after his heart attack told us, "He screamed at the nurses, the doctors, but worst of all he screamed at me. He'd yell, 'Get out. Don't visit. I don't want to see you.' I had very mixed emotions. I was teary. I felt sorry for myself. And I was angry at him. He was making hard times—much harder."

After one woman's hospital stay for a serious liver condition, she would slam the door, turn on the TV, and refuse to talk to anyone.

Each of us reacts to illness according to long-established personality patterns. Our needs, however, become exaggerated. Many patients become demanding, childish, irritable and prone to angry outbursts of temper. The greater the disability, the greater the anger.

The person rendering the care also feels anger. Because of guilt, this anger might not be acknowledged but it may be revealed in forgetting to give the patient medicine, being unavailable for M.D. appointments or by developing an illness of your own.

A Reminder: While psychosomatic diseases may be caused by repressed feelings, these diseases are real and require medical treatment by a physician.

Anger can also cause symptoms almost as debilitating as a real illness. It can make us hypochondriacs. Recent research indicates that the majority of people suffering from imagined symptoms are experiencing emotional problems. Today medical doctors, not psychiatrists, see most of the people with emotional problems. This is probably because psychological problems still connote weakness and loss of face whereas physical complaints are viewed as legitimate. You don't have to have a purse full of pills to be a hypochondriac. Millions of people convince themselves that a small problem—for example, a persistent headache—is really a fatal brain tumor.

A leading internist in New York City told us that women do not express as much anger at illness as men. He felt women were more accepting of disability and limitations because they have less trouble being dependent. He felt his male patients denied illness more and tended to be angrier when ill.

At times of anger, many of us experience an increase in bodily concerns. However, if this becomes an all-pervasive, incapacitating obsession, true hypochondriasis results. Hypochondriacs convert their emotional conflicts into imaginary illness so well they vehemently deny emotional difficulties and usually refuse to see a psychiatrist. While people of any age may become hypochondriacs, this is more common after the age of forty-five.

Dr. Raymond Simon, a New York City internist, told us about a seventy-year-old female patient who, like many hypochondriacs, would eventually get better just to, a few months later, develop another serious illness.

"This seventy-year-old woman first came to see me because she hit her head on a chest of drawers. Immediately, she told me she wanted a skull x-ray. She was positive it was a concussion. She had even convinced herself it was garbling her thinking. While she does have a hiatus hernia, about two months after that incident, she came in sure she had cancer. Once she cut herself and called me positive she had blood poisoning. She has had an unbelievable array of illnesses, but whatever happens, she always thinks the absolute worst. Whenever she becomes 'ill,' she gets very angry, asking over and over, 'Why does this have to happen to me?' All I do is reassure her. But each time, she has to run the gamut—visiting several specialists—before she can be really at ease. Then she becomes less angry and less anxious. But in three months, the cycle begins again."

Hypochondria frequently accompanies depression, an anger turned inward. One researcher found that, out of 234 depressed patients, fifty percent masked their true problem with physical maladies. The hypochondriacal aches and pains in many depressed women appear suddenly, usually over a few weeks. In more serious psychological disturbances—like schizophrenia, for example—the complaints are often bizarre. For example, a woman might believe her bowels are rotting. Such symptoms, especially in a young woman, require immediate attention.

Psychological testing reveals a typical hypochondriac has exaggerated responses to all situations. Even more revealing, as a group, they score below average in self-esteem, a hallmark of people with repressed anger.

"Many hypochondriacs feel they don't deserve friends," explains one New York City psychiatrist. "Illness is the club they use to drive others away. No one can listen to another person's complaints day in and day out."

The connection between physical disease and angry feelings is certainly nothing new. In the 13th century, Henri de Mondeville, a surgeon, noted that negative emotions might interfere with recovery from surgery. He wrote: "The surgeon must forbid anger, hatred and sadness in the patient, and remind him that the body grows fat from joy and thin from sadness."

If you or someone you know has translated anger into an illness, do not conclude it is just "mental." While psychosomatic diseases may be caused by repressed feelings, these diseases are real and require medical treatment by a physician. Unfortunately, you cannot simply think this type of disease away. By learning to deal with our angers openly and honestly, however, doctors say we can improve our chances of staying healthy by over ninety percent.

A WARNING
TAKE CARE OF YOUR HEALTH

When internalized, anger often becomes a serious physical ailment. Immediately after a loss, even if you are the one who left a relationship, there is a greatly increased risk of serious illness. Being extra-conscious of sleep, diet and pampering is important.

A WARNING
DRIVE EXTRA CAREFULLY

A car is a symbol of power. Anger results from powerlessness. The power of the wheel gives us back control. It is no coincidence that many women told me driving fast felt soothing.

One woman who had a near-fatal car accident, breaking her neck and nearly killing herself and her daughter, told me, "I am a fast driver but that morning was different. I was absolutely furious and I took it out on my driving. When I turned the car around, I did it in such a rage, I flipped the car completely over. The car was totalled; I was just lucky we weren't killed. There was no other car involved and I know that accident was one hundred percent due to my anger."

When people are angry, studies show they are definitely more accident-prone. Their reflexes are not as good. It is important that you are aware of this. Driving when angry can be deadly. You may not care at the moment but the consequences for yourself and others can be devastating.

10

When Relationships End

The only relationships we tend to value are those which last, if not forever, at least a long, long time. Ours is a one-and-only, forever-and-ever ethic.

Yet the reality is that for most of us, whether married or single, young or old, fewer and fewer relationships are lasting forever. While years ago people had to deal with the death of a loved one, today we must cope with the fact that many significant people in our lives—mates, friends, lovers—are going to stay alive and that our relationships may die before we do.

In life, each of us fears most three kinds of loss: the loss of love, the loss of control and the loss of esteem. In a death, divorce or parting all these losses occur at once.

When relationships end, we feel an enormous void. We feel our future has been taken from us; we feel our happiness has been taken from us. Kierkegaard, in his essay *The Sickness unto Death*, pinpoints so well the cause of our misery and anger:

"Despair is never ultimately over the external object but always over ourselves. A girl loses her sweetheart and she despairs. It is not over the lost sweetheart but over herself without the sweetheart. And so it is with all cases of loss whether it be money, power or social rank. The unbearable loss is not really in itself unbearable. What we cannot bear is being stripped of the external object. We stand denuded and see the intolerable abyss of ourselves."

Unfortunately, when we are so pained and hurt, we usually find little support. A thirty-year-old divorced woman with three children explained:

"When you find yourself having problems, you also quickly discover you have no one to turn to. You can't go to your friends because they just enjoy the gossip. I really think people enjoy other people's tragedies. You can't turn to your parents because they never really understand and even are likely to say, 'Who told you to get divorced in the first place?' "

Over and over, religious women mentioned that their churches or temples were of no help whatsoever. "The place where I thought I'd get the most support was where I found the least," a church-going Episcopalian who recently divorced said. An orthodox Jewish woman who was divorced said, "They treated me like a pariah, an embarrassment."

We may feel entirely alone but we are not. Millions of women suffer these same feelings each year.

It doesn't take a social scientist to observe that American family life has been undergoing great change. The divorce rate in the United States far exceeds that of any other nation.

Today, the average marriage lasts only 6.8 years. There were 1.18 million divorces in 1979 compared with 395,000 divorces in 1959. According to the National Center of Health Statistics, the number of divorces granted in the U.S. tripled in the last twenty years. And forty-four percent of all remarriages end in divorce. This year, in Los Angeles alone, there are one thousand divorces a week!

The states in which the largest numbers of divorces occurred were California, 137,683; Texas, 92,399; Florida, 69,707; New York, 64,420 and Ohio, 59,548. North Dakota, a state with one of the smallest populations, had the fewest divorces, 2,094 in 1979.

Intimate relationships also end through death. Thousands of women become widows each year. The number of unmarried relationships that end, while not easily documented, is known to be in the thousands too.

Despite the tremendous numbers—approaching a majority—every woman in a broken relationship feels a pit in her stomach and deep anger at her fate.

Anger happens to all of us after a loss. Only how we cope with our anger varies.

Why do some people repress their rage and seem angry forever while others meet the problem head-on without as much *angst*? One answer is personality. People are simply born with different temperaments. All you have to do is watch newborns to see that. Our way of dealing with anger is also copied from our parents.

Primarily, however, our reactions to loss depend on our sense of self. If our loss causes our sense of self to fall into question, our feelings of frustration, helplessness and anger can be intense. Sonya Friedman, a psychologist and marriage and divorce counselor, has said:

"Women have problems with anger because they don't have a sense of security within. Women go from being an extension of their families to being an extension of their husbands. The man usually has more power, so whatever sense of identity she has can easily be snuffed out."

Losses take many forms—death, divorce, the empty nest. Unique to a woman is another loss—the loss of our natural ability to bear a chld. Jennifer, a statuesque, thirty-nine-year-old single actress, confessed that the end of her child-bearing years is a source of tremendous anger. With emotion, she explained:

> "I have a deep inner fear that I may never have a child. I know I could live without a man but not without a child. For me, a child will make me whole. The love of a child is based on true love and I don't want to miss that.
>
> "My anger is based on the fact that my body, my hormones put me in a bind. Things are narrowing down. My biological clock is running out.
>
> "What's interesting is, I don't think about it until that first spot of blood appears each month. I think, 'Here's life draining out of me again; here's fertility leaving my body again.' Then I begin to look around. All the available men are either married, homosexual or much younger. I don't want to have just anyone's child. And all the time, I'm dealing with the clock ticking away. I have tremendous anger. I know it's silly to go around blaming all the homosexuals and all the married men but I can't help myself. I know I don't need a husband. I know I could support a child and I know I could handle the parenting. But the anger is inside to make that decision. I keep waiting and waiting but I know I can't afford to wait. If I wasn't pressured by that clock ticking away—if I knew like men do that I could easily have children for ten more years—I wouldn't be as angry."

We cannot control our emotions any more than we can control our reproductive system. Although we can't control our feelings—they naturally come and go—we can temper their display. Understanding why we feel what we feel, is the first step.

We all have an internal system of "shoulds" and "should nots," says Helen De Rosis, M.D., a psychiatrist at Karen Horney Psychoanalytic Center of Manhattan and author of *Women and Anxiety.* "These expectations are the outcome of what every child thinks her mother and father expect of her but each of us takes these expectations and elaborates on them."

When we set too many standards for ourselves, fulfilling them all becomes impossible. Jennifer was an independent woman yet her traditional "shoulds" were still whispering in her ear. This conflict caused frustration, helplessness and tremendous anger.

As anyone who has been through a divorce knows, divorce can cause intense anger—often more intense than we ever experienced before. The story of Marilyn, a thirty-eight-year-old divorcée with three children who recently completed law school and just married, reflects many of these feelings.

"I went back to school because I got married when I was a junior in college. I had children at an early age and I suddenly realized that the children would be gone and I would still be quite young.

"I decided that if I went to law school it would take only three years and by then Elizabeth would be old enough for me to go to work.

"Ned was very supportive of my going to school. But, once I started going, it was a much heavier commitment than I had ever anticipated. We couldn't lead the same lives we led before simply because I wasn't available. It caused problems.

"I think the first problem was really that I felt all these years, and as I look back I think I exaggerated a lot of it, I had been giving and giving to everybody and now it was my turn. I didn't get the kind of help I felt I deserved. It started off well and then things kind of fell apart, and I was going to school full time with lots of homework, and keeping house and doing all the finances for the house. Ned was finding it very difficult to try to cope with these things; when he tried to help, he found that difficult. I always found it difficult to ask other people to do things for me so I wasn't asking, and he wasn't doing, then he'd try to do it and he'd get frustrated, and then he'd get angry and then I'd get angry.

"I think school changed the pattern of my life that I'd lived with for many years. It made me aware of things I had been unhappy about for many years. If I had expressed those feelings earlier, they could have been dealt with. I think it goes back to the whole idea of my trying to be nice to everybody all the time because that's the way you're brought up to be.

"My second year Ned started off trying to be very good and very helpful, but it all fell apart, and I got very upset and somehow I just kept feeling unhappy.

"The difficulty I have now is that I never went as far as I should have in identifying exactly what it was that I was so unhappy about. I have always been very good, proper, and judgmental of other people—everything had to be *right*, so for me to have moved out and left my family, I must have really been in bad shape. I don't think I even stopped to think. I was running without knowing what I was doing.

"The anger took me over physically. It got so bad, it was a very physical feeling. I just had to go. During the time we were separated, my anger was shut off—I just didn't think about it. That was totally unrealistic. And then, we decided to divorce.

"I wasn't really angry that the divorce happened 'cause I was the one who wanted it. It was very hard and very painful and more painful afterwards because when you're cooler and you look back, you can see all your mistakes. Although I was terribly unhappy, I feel guilty because I see that if I'd dealt with things more we could have worked it out.

"My anger took different forms. During the first year I cried a lot. Later on, I seemed to stop eating. I lost a lot of weight. Then I turned off my feelings. I was scared a lot of the time. I knew I could take care of myself, but I feared loneliness. There were times when my apartment was fun—like coming home and turning on the TV and having my dinner. But, if the phone didn't ring, I'd have to call someone. I couldn't stand it after having been used to bedlam for so long.

"One evening when I was here and he was here—I think it was shortly before we both got married—he said something that made me so mad that I went at him and I think I would have hit him. He backed away and in a few minutes we were both laughing and he said, 'I was really afraid of you!' And I said, 'Boy, if I had only done that a long time ago.'

"I was wild, and I'd never felt that way before. It was a good feeling, in a way, to feel that anger. I think that I probably never did handle anger in a constructive way.

"When I get angry now, I say something. Jack's wonderful and we've talked a lot about all these things I've said. He's anxious for me to talk to him. If I feel a certain way, he wants to hear about it. Somehow this has been a purge from the shell I was living in before—in every way doing what was expected of me. I don't feel I have to show a particular face to the world. There's a great freedom in that which relieves me of a burden I've carried since I was a little girl. I'm much more relaxed and free to be myself."

Marilyn's feelings are familiar to us all but they produced an anger-inducing pattern. She said what she always said; he said what he always said. Each felt helpless to change things and people are angered by helplessness.

Marilyn and Ned also misunderstood each other's problems, a very common difficulty in many marriages. We must remember that everyone sees the world through different eyes. When people view issues differently, they can easily become polarized, unless they make a real effort to see what the other person is seeing. Laura Singer, co-author of *States: The Crises That Shape Your Marriage*, has said, "All kinds of needless misunderstandings can be avoided by asking yourself, 'Where is he coming from?' 'What is he really trying to tell me?'"

More than anything, however, Marilyn's accumulated rage

was probably due to years and years of repression. Repression has been taught to little girls for so long, it often becomes automatic. Again and again, psychiatrists stress the importance of verbalizing your feelings. The reason the traditional cartoon of the husband who comes home, drinks a beer and silently reads the newspaper causes such rage in the wife is because neither husband nor wife is expressing himself or herself.

For a woman, the death of a mother is another particularly painful and anger-inducing experience no matter when it strikes. If the mother dies when a child is young, the hurt is more intense. A fifty-three-year-old nursery school teacher told us:

> "My mother died when I was eighteen and she was forty. I was very angry and to this day I still feel the loss. I think my life turned dramatically because of my mother's death.
>
> "I was married at eighteen but after my mother died, I divorced immediately and married my boss. Our marriage has lasted but Joseph is twenty years older than me. I don't think I would have married a parent figure if my mother hadn't died.
>
> "My mother always seemed to me omnipotent. She was president of the PTA, chairman of this organization and that one. She seemed like she could control everything. All of a sudden, she wasn't there for me. She wasn't coming with me to buy my dresses like she was supposed to. I missed her tremendously. For a year, I wore black.
>
> "Throughout my life, my sense of loss and anger keeps coming back. When my daughter was born, it seemed to me everyone had their mothers around. Here I had this beautiful, precocious child and no one to show her to. Of course I had compassion for my mother when she was ill, but most of all I was angry."

When we have experienced the loss of a loved one, no words can really ease the pain. Friends don't know what to do or say, and so may avoid you. A forty-nine-year-old widow, a book editor said, "When people saw me, they'd actually cross the street. They just did not want to face me." What can friends do? Rather than advice, some questions may be more helpful. For example, "Is there someone else you would like me to call?" "Do you feel like talking about it?" "I am not sure how I might help. Is there anything I can do for you?"

A divorce or death is a major loss and we grieve. Elizabeth Kubler-Ross identified the stages we all go through in grief.

DENIAL: The first stage after any loss is denial. Denial is an important protective device, but most people quickly move on to the second step, depression.

DEPRESSION: When you see that you have lost a relationship and maybe a lifestyle, a home, a dream and a family besides, there is always depression. You may feel it is more than you can stand. The situation is hopeless. There is nothing you can do, nothing anyone can do.

ANGER: Anger is the stage that follows depression. (Usually people flip-flop from anger one day to depression the next.) When we realize our future has been taken from us, we naturally feel tremendous anger. Our rage at our fate and feeling of impotence to change things is often displaced onto friends and relatives. (They should not take this personally but should try to understand that, in a similar position, they undoubtedly would be angry too.)

REEVALUATION AND READJUSTMENT: This fourth and final stage is not easily arrived at. If the relationship has been a long and very significant one, this stage can take a number of years. At this stage, you are able to look at your life and your relationships from a different perspective.

While these stages are demarcated for professional purposes, most people do not progress in strict order and do not move through all the stages. They may stay in a particular stage depending on their personality. For example, if somebody has been angry all their life, they are more likely to stay in the anger stage. Indeed, the goal should not be to push a person through the stages but to reach a stage where they are comfortable.

No intimate relationship ends with just a momentary pang. There is always a tremendous amount of anguish and great pain. Anger is always present due to: disappointment, loss of control, loneliness, a loss of self-esteem, a sense of uncertainty.

While these factors can lead to extreme anger, it is important to remember that no action to end a relationship should be taken in anger. When one has taken a stand in anger saying, "I'll never sleep with you again," or, "I'm moving out," a woman sometimes feels it is a loss of face to change her mind. Pride can make her live up to a hasty declaration.

One psychologist told us that women, more than men, are angry due to disappointment. Even before entering a serious relationship, a woman may already look to change her partner—nothing big, just this *one* little thing. The truth is people change very little, so many women end up angry— angry at themselves because they knew these things in the first place, angry at their partner because he hasn't changed and angry at those around them because they are not helping.

All of us direct our lives according to mental images. If we never saw ourselves in the role of divorcée, widow or frustrated mother, the anger will be even greater.

Many women have been encouraged by what they have read and seen on television to strike out on their own. But they have no inkling of the inner turmoil that sudden aloneness after years of marriage can produce.

Both men and women are often disappointed at what their new life brings. Available single companions are often harder to find than imagined. The single life is not what they hoped. "I've gone through all that hell of the divorce just to get to this," said one angry and hurt thirty-three-year-old divorcée. "It wasn't worth it."

A relationship may end although we do not want it to, causing us to feel helpless, out of control. Therefore, we may desperately seek a new relationship. "If only I could find someone to love me again, I would be happy," many women feel. Unfortunately, meeting someone is not entirely in our control.

And there may be problems even if we do "meet somebody." We may find he is not as we hoped. We then feel disillusioned. Again we become desperate, and so it goes. It takes all our energy and it only intensifies our anger.

Usually when a marriage or love affair ends, one party is taken more by surprise. What happens has been compared to termites eating away a house. All of a sudden, so it seems, the foundation collapses. Somewhere between the arguments over bills and missing emotional support, destructive patterns develop. When we know what to expect, we can prepare ourselves emotionally. If loss catches us by surprise, we begin to doubt ourselves and our judgments.

Coping with loneliness is probably the most difficult of all our tasks after a meaningful relationship ends.

According to Allan Fromme in *The Ability to Love*, "True loneliness is a basic sense of unconnectedness with people. It is in essence the denial of satisfaction of a deep need that we all share, the need to form relationships, to become attached, to love and be loved in some way."

Each family develops its own private rituals, a unique blend which we describe as "home." While it may be composed of unconscious things, it is a feeling we know and so do our children. A divorce, death or separation disrupts this family feeling. Its absence makes people feel lost and immeasurably alone.

Increasing the number of people that make you happy is another way to feel less lonely. We are liable to be extremely lonely if we depend on only one person—a husband, boyfriend or lover—for happiness. Obviously, we are vulnerable if we lose that one source. A young woman who was divorced after four years of marriage explained, "I felt so ashamed. My husband didn't want me. There was another woman involved. And I was so unsuspecting. I thought my marriage was just fine. I was hit like a ton of bricks. I was totally unprepared. People like me didn't get divorced. My husband was everything to me—friend, lover, confidant. I had no outside interests, and no other close friends. I was so alone and so excruciatingly lonely."

Increasing the number of skills we know—for example, learning to water-ski, type, do needlepoint or read a stock market report—is also important. This gives a sense of accomplishment and also increases security. As psychiatrist Dr. Maynard Shelly explained, "The power to control your environment helps to keep you happy. A feeling of control is one of the most important bases for optimism."

While self-help books advocate all sorts of activities, most are impossible for the truly lonely person. Studies show that lonely women do participate in social acitivities. Unfortunately, participation never results in real enjoyment. This might not be apparent to the casual observer but psychiatric interviews show these women feel uneasy, supersensitive and uncomfortable.

One thing which does enhance meaningful social contacts is getting a person to speak about themselves. No matter how different people are, this inevitably brings out things in common. We tend to feel most comfortable with others of common interests and experiences.

Ending an intimate relationship produces a feeling of failure. No matter what our role, we inevitably blame ourselves. Jocelyn, a Princeton college junior whose boyfriend just ended their nine-month relationship, commented:

"You are a different person when you are involved. You are confident on your own. You depend on yourself. It's different when you are waiting for someone to call, waiting for them to say, 'I like you.'

"There are all these questions you worry about. 'Did I say the right thing?' 'Will he call?' 'Shall I go to his room?' You are always wondering, 'Am I doing the right thing?' 'Am I being too aggressive?' 'Not aggressive enough?' When Jared broke up with me, all I could think was that I should have known better. Why did I expose myself? Why did I bring this on myself?

"Honestly, I don't know where to turn. I'm talkative. I talk to my sister, to my friends. The more I talk, I feel I will let the hurt out and it will go away. But it does not really work. The hurt is still there.

"I feel rejected. No matter what he said, and he was very nice about it, I feel if I had been just a little prettier and more casual, we would still be together.

"I don't want to lose my self-confidence...to lower myself in my own eyes. But it's happening, no matter how hard I try to talk myself out of it. When I see my friends who are engaged or have steady relationships, I'm jealous. Sometimes I wonder what's wrong with me, when is all this going to end so I don't have to worry about loneliness and don't have to ask all those questions anymore."

When someone rejects us, we begin to believe the rejection. We feel, "If he did it, I must deserve it." Nowhere is the ego defeat and rejection greater than during divorce. Although rationally we know some marriages should end, we do not excuse ourselves easily. The mental if-onlys go on and on: "If only he hadn't..." "If only I had..."

Long-forgotten episodes keep coming up for mental review, touching and releasing long-suppressed stories of emotions. A forty-five-year-old divorced woman said, "After twenty years of marriage, I found myself recalling things sixteen or seventeen years old. I remembered the time we argued right after our wedding. I remember how I felt all alone during the birth of our first child. Feelings welled up in me as if it were yesterday. I cried about them all over again. Then I got angry. I could see those early signs were all indications of what was to come. On the one hand, these rememberances gave me insight but they also confused and angered me. Why hadn't I spoken up? Why had I gone on to have more children? Why was I always so afraid and dependent?"

Although divorce is common today, society still considers it somewhat of a stigma. When we are stigmatized, we undergo a loss of self-esteem and confidence.

Saying goodbye to an old relationship means saying hello to an uncertain future. For women (and men, too) this causes anxiety. Many new decisions must be made. Where do I want to live? What do I really want to do with the rest of my life? What is really best for my children? Myself?

Ambivalence, indecision and fear surround any change. So, inevitably, there is anger that we are forced to grapple with these difficulties.

"When I was married, I had a good idea of what was expected of me," a forty-year-old woman, divorced after twelve years of marriage, remarked. "But now that I am divorced I'm never sure what is expected of me. This is a whole new world to me. I'm never sure how to act or what to do."

When guidelines are gone, our feelings—usually our anger— may become our guiding force. While understandable, this is not in our best interest.

Anger is painful to ourselves as well as others. We may wish to overlook our anger and avoid the pain of an early experience half-remembered. Unfortunately, we pay a price when we do this. Someone who habitually inhibits her feelings of anger loses touch not only with the emotion but also with a sense of when anger is appropriate. She sees a threat everywhere fearing her anger may emerge. She is ever on guard lest someone, anyone, surprise her into revealing her inner turmoil.

Some people go to the opposite extreme, erupting in anger frequently. These people may justify their anger by glorifying it. A lot of people who are demonstratively angry flatter themselves that they are passionate. Passion and anger are not the same. Passion is the mobilization of energies and intelligence in the direction of a goal while anger has more to do with feelings of frustration and helplessness.

Irrational as it may be, the departure from our lives of one who provided physical and emotional care inevitably produces intense feelings of anger. This is true of all endings—even if we *wanted* the divorce—indeed even death. "How dare he die and leave me in this miserable mess?" is our feeling. We blame him for creating our present misery. Because we know these thoughts are irrational, we may deny them. But denying them will not make them go away. Indeed, it may make them more destructive.

The power of emotion we feel when a loved one leaves us began with our fear, as a child, of being abandoned. We never outgrow it. We feel we cannot survive.

Separation anxiety occurs when children are separated from their parents or when anyone is separated from anything symbolizing security. In normal development, these fears are gradually replaced by feelings of trust and self-sufficiency. Yet some children find that going to school or camp produces unbearable anxiety. (Degrees of separation anxiety vary.) Any new loss reawakens these early fears. One should remember, however, that some separation anxiety is normal; it is impossible to prevent all the anxiety involved in ending a comfortable situation and beginning the unknown.

When angers envelope us, we do not know how to regain our

emotional strength. Dr. Ned Marcus, a New York City psychiatrist, shared with us some of his thoughts:

"I feel there has been too much emphasis on the positive and redeeming aspects of the free expression of anger. We do not automatically feel better by expressing anger. Indeed we may feel worse. Often the free expression of anger exacerbates problems. All that happens is you get yourself all upset and you irritate others. The trick is to somehow deal with the inevitable frustrations of life in a constructive way.

"Of course, people will say, 'I have a *right* to get angry,' but my response is always, 'Yes, but will it do any good?' Especially after a divorce, a woman may feel she has been cheated by her spouse. She has a strong sense of entitlement and justice. Over and over she will ask, 'Wasn't that unfair?' In many cases, they are right. They were wronged. They have been cheated. But does it help to rage against it? Could they do something better?

"This is not an ideal world. Most people are treated unfairly during a divorce. I try to direct them to new understandings, new strategies. It may sound, at first, like a therapy of resignation but it is not. It can be very productive because it enables a person to find alternatives. They are no longer as frustrated. Many people get so stuck in the anger itself, it is extremely difficult to 'unstick' them.

"By changing the framework of a problem, you can change a person's perception. This can be immensely helpful in dealing with anger."

How can we manage our anger with more satisfying results? Advice is easy to give. Under the stress of outside difficulties and personality conflicts, it can be nearly impossible to follow. These suggestions, obtained from women themselves as well as professionals, may help return our sense of power, giving us new paths out of our anger trap.

1. *Don't take things personally.* Dr. Ned Marcus suggests,

"Think of how this person has acted in other situations. You will probably realize his actions resulted more from him than from you. It is easier for us to be accepting when we don't take things personally."

2. *Make short-term not permanent changes.* When angry, this is not the time to "settle things once and for all." The unevenness of a crisis lends itself to a healthy fear of long-term permanent decisions. The best alternative is to start with short-term, temporary decisions and reevaluate.

3. *Dream, dream, dream.* Dreams are a way of releasing suppressed anger. When angry, we may fantasize doing something cruel to a mate, parent or child. Such daydreams are not rare. Freud believed dreams were a safety valve through which our darkest impulses could escape harmlessly.

Some professionals actually suggest fantasizing the very worst. Psychiatrist Walter Reich of the National Institute of Mental Health points out, "You are allowed to think anything without feeling guilty; fantasies never hurt anybody." A young writer told us she fantasized flattening her lover, throwing him into her typewriter, and then typing him into a thousand tiny pieces. A mother told us she fantasized putting her children into an institution so she would not have to care for them anymore. Interestingly, the majority of us *do* think terrible thoughts; only a very very few put them into action. (And this is *not* recommended!)

4. *Leave the situation.* Sometimes it is best to realize that you feel angry but you must avoid a confrontation. One woman told us, "When my ex-husband comes over and we start fighting about our son, sometimes I just can't take it. Our son has a learning disability and we have always disagreed on how he should be handled. Now I will say, 'I don't want to listen anymore because you are making me very angry so I am going to leave this room.' And I do. It makes me feel better." Fleeing—away for a weekend, out for lunch or just out of a

room—reenergizes a person. At the very least it puts you out of range and consequently less likely to say something you'll later regret.

5. *Keep past romances private*. As new relationships develop, many women feel this warm and trusting feeling and so the confidences commence. "I want to tell them what I've been through—about all the abortions and near-suicides and agony," said one too-candid woman. "I want them to know how much I've overcome in order to give them a sense of my worth, to point out how strength of character and brain power have seen me through. However, after giving a recital of the hurts inflicted by other men, I've never yet had a man say, 'I'm proud of you for living through such ordeals. You must be a splendid person.' Instead, they hoard all this stuff and then when the relationship has developed a few wrinkles and we're not getting along quite so beautifully, they drag this privileged information out and use it against me. A man will say something like, 'You're just blaming me for what that guy in Seattle did to you.' "

A thirty-eight-year-old advertising executive explained, "Joe reacted with great sympathy and understanding when I told him about my two-year love affair with a married man, but later when I found out he was having an affair with another woman, his reply was, 'Who are you to talk to me about faithfulness? You went out with a married man.' "

While you might think that psychiatrists would sympathize with great openness, few do. Professionals feel such honesty is hurtful and insensitive. In this age of sexual sophistication and marital break-ups, many people come to each other with a past. But knowing every detail of it will not bring you closer.

As Laura Singer, Ed.D., past President of the American Association for Marriage and Family Therapy, has said, "Although honesty is an ideal, to be honest at *all* times is really to act out a lot of aggression and hostility. You have to consider what the impact of what is said will be upon your partner."

6. *Forget the past: confine yourself to the here and now.* It is past resentments which cause our rage and conflicts. We dwell on the trait that is being shown rather than the present problem. One way of by-passing these difficulties is to confine present discussions to one issue. Stick to that issue rather than what is wrong with your ex-intimate. Of course this requires a constant effort and is immensely difficult to do. But it will be easier if you limit discussion time. And remember, the past is something that can never be changed despite your feelings. It's over and being angry will not change a thing.

7. *Don't try to be the winner.* In a difficult interpersonal conflict both people either win or both are the losers. Your goal should be to improve an upsetting situation, not to gain revenge. The point is not to make the other person feel bad or guilty—nor to prove you are right—but to improve the relationship.

These suggestions may be helpful; they are not magical cures. Anger lasts. Some psychiatrists suggest that with every major loss the anger lasts at least five years and often as much as ten years.

As Dr. Theodore I. Rubin points out in his excellent book *Compassion and Self-Hate*, "If we are going to live as human beings on earth rather than gods in some imaginary kingdom, then we're going to come face to face with painful losses and disappointments: lose people we love, fail at goals that mean everything to us. There isn't even a question of being equipped to deal because we are never adequately prepared for the onslaughts life brings us."

The secret to happy relations, then, seems to be in the way we approach and handle the things that do come along in our life. Depending on our outlook and our freedom to express ourselves honestly, we can diminish or intensify the problems that do confront us in life.

The writer Elizabeth Bowen, during a television interview, spoke for all of us looking for the energy and courage to come through a hard time. She had already lost her husband of thirty years and given up her home in Ireland, the one place on earth that meant the most to her. Her health was only fair. When the interviewer asked how she managed to keep going, to keep writing and keep encouraging others, she replied, "I think the main thing, don't you, is to keep the show on the road."

11

A Stronger Self

A nger is not irrational. The immediate cause of our anger is almost always hurt. Present hurt reminds us of deep hurts from our past. No one wants to feel emotional pain. Rather than do so, some people try to anesthetize painful feelings. The most destructive yet commonest ways of escaping uncomfortable feelings of anger are drugs and alcohol.

Most drug users and alcohol abusers are not even consciously angry. They may use these substances to feel more comfortable with themselves. Unfortunately substances cannot give us self-confidence or a stronger ego. What's worse, they do just the opposite. Drugs anesthetize all feelings. One drug user who was kind and thoughtful off drugs but stole from friends and family while on drugs explained, "When I use drugs, I have no conscience. All my feelings towards others slip away. I have only one concern—the drugs."

Addiction is devastating for anyone, but its physical and

social effect on women is particularly severe. A June, 1982 survey by *Redbook Magazine* of more than 62 agencies in 38 states who worked with more than 11,000 women showed that women suffer more both physically and socially from alcohol. Alcoholic women may develop cirrhosis of the liver faster than men; they may damage their reproductive capacity as well as harm unborn children.

Socially, alcoholic women are more often dismissed from jobs than alcoholic men, and when their alcoholism is discovered, men are more likely to abandon alcoholic wives than the reverse.

It is unwise to generalize about addiction. Each person's story is unique. We spoke with two women who tried this escape route. Here are their stories:

Jennifer, an attractive blond, comes from an esteemed professional family.

"I grew up in an upper-middle-class, white, rural area. My parents would always say, 'You have the best, this is the best school, we live in the best house.' I never had to struggle or fight for anything because they gave me everything I ever wanted.

"I was very angry, though. I felt my life was too controlled. I was told just what to do, when to do my homework, and which boy was alright to go out with and which wasn't.... But I kept seeing the one who wasn't anyway. When I was in high school, I was already very rebellious. I loved to drink a lot. I was into jazz and Beat things.

"I got pregnant towards the end of high school. I gave the child up for adoption. They convinced me to. They felt it was a stigma (of course I didn't care about the stigma) but I couldn't care for the child. Now I'm angry about having given that child up. If I hadn't I'd have a daughter sixteen now. I didn't have the pleasure of seeing her grow up, maybe I would have grown up too.

"I got into the Flower Era in college. It seemed whenever I sat down to tell my father about it he'd always strike me down. 'You'll get over it; you'll see what is right,' was his answer to everything. He never, for one moment, considered that what I was saying might be valid too. He'd always tear me down. I'd leave home feeling very bewildered.

"I was always getting money from them. Most of it, though, I used for drugs. I started with alcohol, then pot, then acid, mescaline and finally even heroin. It began in high school. All the kids were getting high. In college it continued. When I moved to Oregon for graduate school, I started using heroin. I was always attracted to the drug culture. All my friends were artists or jazz musicians.

"I felt, here are all these down people. I wanted to be like them. Everyone I knew was using drugs. I wanted to be there too. I was enraptured by the drug world.

"I started living with a black man. We were using drugs. Then I felt anger towards him too. Here I was being so adventurous, but he always insisted on getting the drugs. He made me stay home. It was all so middle class. To my parents, I pretended he was going to law school. Of course he never was.

"It made me feel like I was charting my life to be in that segment. It gave me a direction, something to do. When I was first using drugs, I showed everyone the tracks on my arm. I was honestly proud of them.

"I was painting at the time. On drugs I did some really nice things. I remember one self-portrait I did. It shows a black man playing the flute. I was a reflection in the mirror. I don't think I really had a separate identity.

"Now I want to go into a treatment center and eventually put together a book of all my work.

"But if I had to do it all again, I wouldn't do it differently. I think I learned a lot. I know everything about this culture.

"Sometimes I think I was pushed into it all because I wasn't allowed to raise my child alone. But I really know I did it to myself."

Odessa, a thirty-three-year-old single black woman, has a fourteen-year-old son.

"I think my anger comes from all the hurt in my life. My father was a homosexual. He tried to cover it up of course. But I always knew. More than anything, it confused me. Why was my father like that? I kept trying to figure it out but I still can't understand it.

"I had an uncle who molested me when I was eleven. He sat me on his penis. He fondled my breasts even though I really didn't have any, you know, just those little buds. He was intoxicated when he did it but my Mom went crazy when she found out. He never penetrated me. But I never forgot it. What's worse, my Mom never really explained it to me.

"When I was eighteen, I had an affair with a boy I really liked. When I told him I was pregnant, he was gone like a flash of light. That still triggers anger in me. My son is fourteen now and I hate to admit it but sometimes I look at my son and I'll see his father and get enraged all over again.

"I didn't use drugs until I was twenty-one. I was going to college. The guy that gave me a ride to school got me into it. People would tell me I did drugs because I had an inferiority complex. But it wasn't that to me. It was the anger about all those incidents. The anger was pounding in my head. I felt like one of those pressure-cookers. I felt if I didn't do drugs I'd do something really insane like murder someone, or something really awful like you read in the newspapers. It was this or go crazy. When you're high, you don't feel mad. It calmed me down.

"Drugs feel like orgasm. You get a fantastic relief of tension, a total release. But the side effects are hell.

"Because my anger involved other people, I could not seem to solve it. I was frustrated. Nothing helped.

"To this day, I don't know how to deal with it all but I know drugs aren't the answer. What I think would help me is having somebody, a companion. I wish I had somebody who would take the time to help me put this puzzle together; someone I could share honestly with and know that it wouldn't be used against me later; somebody who doesn't just want my body or my money or someone to get high with. Someone who honestly cares."

Dr. Madelaine Amiel, Assistant Professor of Chemical Psychiatry at Mount Sinai Medical School and Unit Director for the Female Ward at Bernstein Institute, the largest drug detoxification service in New York City, explained, "Many of these women use drugs to appease all sorts of uncomfortable emotional feelings—anxiety, depression, anger. They simply cannot tolerate this level of emotional distress. It is very easy to seek relief in this way. The neurological system tends to repeat what is pleasurable. Once they take drugs, they enjoy the feelings of relief. A biochemical dependency results."

Since we all have anger, anxiety and depression, why do certain people seek a drug outlet? we asked Dr. Amiel.

"There are many factors, our culture, peer pressure, perhaps a genetic predisposition, less tolerance for emotional pain, childhood scars. But why one person takes drugs and another never does, no one really knows."

Is psychotherapy used to treat this problem? Dr. Amiel explained:

"Beating the addiction, not psychotherapy, is the first and foremost method of treatment. If you did individual therapy, you would have to do it twenty-four hours a day and they would still have their habit. After their detoxification, they must go into a therapeutic community or methadone program with counseling where they receive around-the-clock support and treatment for their drug hunger. Our group therapy sessions give women an opportunity to ventilate their feelings and learn about these programs."

Ventilating our anger is important; gaining insight is crucial. Neither is enough, however, we must become more assertive; we must learn to like ourselves better; we must become more active.

Needless to say, these things are not done easily or quickly. But any change—even a very small one—can make an enormous difference in the quality of a person's life.

A forty-six-year-old mother of four explained:

"In the last year, I've started expressing to my husband feelings I always had but never expressed. Once I got started, it was easier to do. As I was expressing my feelings, I found I had a lot less anger. My husband found it very difficult in the beginning. Then there were periods of great understanding. Then there were times of no understanding at all. It was tough and it is still not over. But even he says, things are much better—I think more real—than before."

A thirty-eight-year-old sculptress told us:

"I have a very thin face. Of all my traits, I think this is my least favorite. I have an aunt who, every time she sees me, says, 'Are you feeling okay? Your face, it looks so thin.' Without fail she makes me seethe with rage."

We all feel rage at such situations because we do not speak up or stand up for ourselves. We feel helpless and diminished in our own eyes. What can we do instead? What would be healthier? One therapist recommended these words, "I love you dearly, Aunt, but when you comment on my appearance like that it really annoys me. Please don't do it."

Traditionally, women have been taught to placate, keep the peace. We do it at work as well as home. Studies show that in meetings involving men and women, women talk less than men, offer fewer opinions, interrupt less often and permit themselves to be interrupted more. It is not that we don't have the ability to assert ourselves, but we are afraid to appear unfeminine and bossy.

Most of all, we are afraid of not being liked. An associate editor commented, "I was constantly tense. I worried about what my husband thought of me, what my boss thought of me, what the other editors thought of me, even the impression I was making on the supermarket check-out girl. Carrying around all this tension not only made me exhausted, it made me angry."

Asserting ourselves does not always please others. It may antagonize at times. Making an enemy may not be as terrible as you fear. Letting others know your limits and feelings will have many benefits. It clearly shows you are a unique individual with rights and feelings. Speaking up is awkward and difficult but each act of assertion makes the next one easier. It is a positive sign of personal growth.

Self-hatred is perhaps the greatest cause of anger. While many women feel disliked, it is actually they who dislike themselves. As Dr. Helen De Rosis states in *The Book of Hope*, "Friends and family members may criticize her, but there is no one who will be able to 'put her down' more critically and more devastatingly than herself. Self-hatred not only keeps us chronically disappointed but angry."

None of us will always be happy or completely satisfied with the way our lives are going. But many people have such negative attitudes towards themselves and such unrealistically high standards that whatever they have accomplished never seems as important as what they haven't. Mary Evans, a thirty-six-year-old product manager, was a perfect example. She explained:

"No matter what I achieve, it seems there is always one thing that makes me unhappy. When I was in college—I felt badly because I wasn't in a good college like all my sisters. After college I worked extremely hard and finally got a good job. But I still inwardly felt like a reject because I didn't have a boyfriend. I thought there was really only one thought in people's minds. 'Poor Mary, she can't get a man.' Finally I got married. Was I happy? Of course, in some ways. But I still felt uneasy. I wasn't yet settled into a home. Then we bought a darling little house. I thought, at last I'd be happy. But we began fixing up the house. The job got botched over and over. I hated the final product. So again, I wasn't at peace. It seemed no matter how fast I raced, how hard I worked, I never could get there."

Perhaps as children we were not praised enough. Whatever the reason, such continual self-punishment is harmful. This kind of thinking shuts off an important source of self-esteem. Your message to yourself should be, for example, "I did all the food shopping and made a nice dinner for the family," not, "I made a good dinner but now the house is dirty and the wash still needs folding and I didn't write Tommy's note." While all this may be true, such an attitude dooms us to continual failure because life's tasks are never finished.

Understanding and dealing with our anger relieve much excessive self-criticism. Dealing effectively with anger is also an antidote to emotional chaos bringing back a sense of direction and order.

Active sports also provide an excellent release for accumulated anger. Sports enhance rather than sap energy. They have a distinct relaxing effect. An interior decorator commented, "I've never been particularly athletic but I tried tennis about five years ago and just love it. Tennis relaxes me. I make a special point of scheduling a game every Sunday evening. Since tennis requires total concentration, there's no place for other concerns. After Sunday's game, I work fresh on Monday without held-over angers from the week before."

One woman, married forty-four years, felt walking was the secret of her successful marriage. She explained that when she and her husband got into a heated argument, each would immediately leave the house and walk around the neighborhood for an hour. This break, combined with exercise, made it easier to resolve differences.

Picking a sport you like is extremely important. Otherwise it might increase frustration. Some women who are poor athletes or have poor coordination may find sports just add to their self-doubts. For them, other activities can serve the same purpose. One woman found a Chinese cooking course great therapy. "The instructor told us that making 'hack chicken' was a great way to vent your anger," she explained. "Yesterday, I tried it and you know what? He was right." One woman even admitted she enjoyed mowing the lawn because it was such a great anger release.

Leonard Berkowitz, a psychologist at the University of Wisconsin, has pointed out that the level of activity is not, as commonly viewed, that important. Active sports *do* make angry people feel less angry, Dr. Berkowitz explains, but only because concentrating on—and physically enjoying the activity—takes the mind off their problems. "Anger will dissolve equally well during a sedentary chess game," he pointed out.

No anger technique is totally effective until we are happy in a relationship. This is not necessarily male/female. One widow explained that after her husband's death, she was constantly with her widowed sister. They confided and supported one another emotionally. For most young women, however, this does mean a man. "If you have love in your life," Ann Landers has said, "it can make up for a great many things you lack. If you don't have it, no matter what else there is, it's not enough."

However, a stronger self means wanting, not needing a man: knowing that when the chips are down, we can survive emotionally on our own.

One woman who remarried at age fifty after twenty years as a single divorcée commented:

> "I don't need a man to make me whole or secure so I am not mad at them for failing me. I know I can support myself and I can survive emotionally. For me, it's not a matter of *need*; it's a matter of like. I like some men; I don't like some. But I'm not disappointed, disillusioned or angry that they aren't doing what I need them to do for me."

We may deeply desire a new relationship. Getting one, however, is more difficult for a woman than a man. Socially it is still a man's world. The physical traces of experience that are prized in men are considered unattractive and undesirable in women.

According to the U.S. Bureau of Census in 1975, seventy-five percent of women who had remarried were divorced from their first husbands before the age of thirty. Only thirty-two percent of women who were divorced in their forties remarried and of women whose marriages ended between the ages of fifty and seventy-five, only twelve percent married again. By the age of about forty-five, nearly twice as many divorced men have married again as women.

As is the case with divorce, fewer widows remarry than widowers. Nearly twice as many men as women remarry within five years of the death of their wives.

After even the most difficult divorce, even the most tragic death, the pain of parting eventually lessens.

We must believe in the ability of time itself to help us forget past pain and rekindle our interest in the future. Part of time's healing power is the human body's unrelenting drive toward physical and emotional health. Life goes on and we survive, sometimes in spite of ourselves.

Coming to an awareness of our feelings and the meanings they hold for us is crucial if we are to make the most of our lives. Grievances from the past can keep affecting us years later. To get on with the future, we must acknowledge the past but then let go of it. This is certainly not easy. But it is the only way to really resolve the real cause of our anger and move on to fresh beginnings.

Epilogue:
Remembering Irene, Josh and Judy

It seems only appropriate to end this book as it began—with Irene, Josh and Judy. I saw the suicide note Irene left. It told how Irene loved her Dad. But most of all, she loved her children. She could not bear to leave them behind. Like most women who suppress their anger, Irene was, even in the end, acting out of love.

If there was a single theme throughout the scores of intimate interviews I conducted for this book, it was that women hide their anger for one overwhelming reason: fear of the loss of love. It is my heartfelt hope that this book makes women appreciate that an honest expression of all feelings, even anger, will not destroy, but enhance, love.